Eyewitness
HORSE

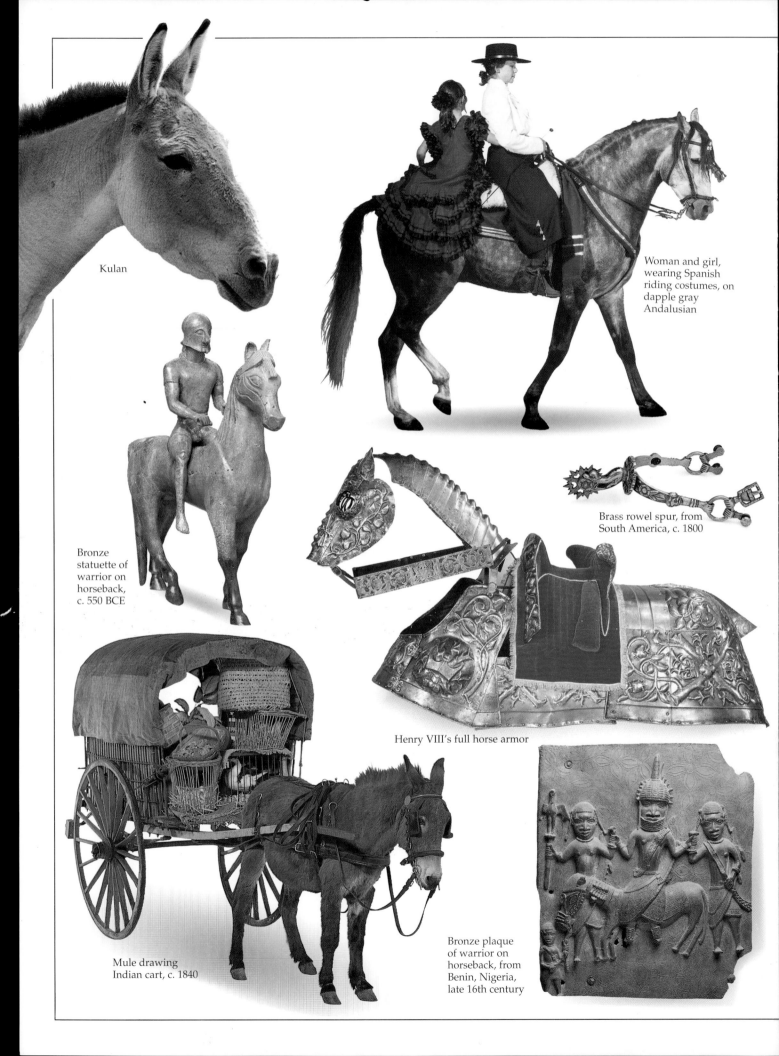

Kulan

Woman and girl, wearing Spanish riding costumes, on dapple gray Andalusian

Bronze statuette of warrior on horseback, c. 550 BCE

Brass rowel spur, from South America, c. 1800

Henry VIII's full horse armor

Mule drawing Indian cart, c. 1840

Bronze plaque of warrior on horseback, from Benin, Nigeria, late 16th century

Foot and two side toes of *Anchitherium* fossil

Eyewitness
HORSE

Old shoe and nails removed from horse's hoof

Written by
JULIET
CLUTTON-BROCK

Mountain zebra

Shoeing a Shire horse

Dapple gray jumping

DK

DK Publishing, Inc.

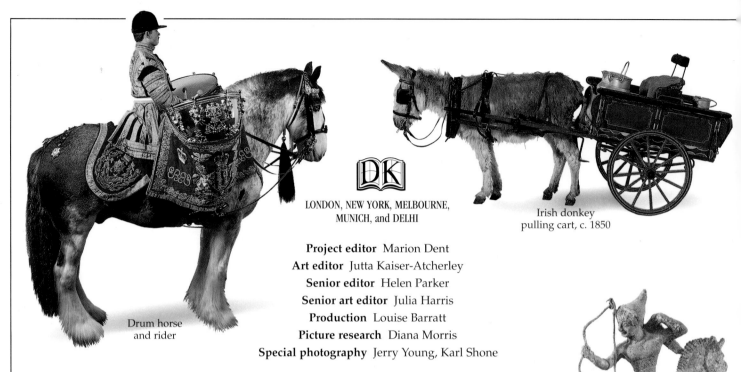

Drum horse
and rider

Two wild Przewalski horses

Irish donkey
pulling cart, c. 1850

DK

LONDON, NEW YORK, MELBOURNE,
MUNICH, and DELHI

Project editor Marion Dent
Art editor Jutta Kaiser-Atcherley
Senior editor Helen Parker
Senior art editor Julia Harris
Production Louise Barratt
Picture research Diana Morris
Special photography Jerry Young, Karl Shone

REVISED EDITION
Managing editor Andrew Macintyre
Managing art editor Jane Thomas
Editor and reference compiler Susan Malyan
Art editor Rebecca Johns
Production Jenny Jacoby
Picture research Bridget Tily
DTP designer Siu Yin Ho

U.S. editor Elizabeth Hester
Senior editor Beth Sutinis
Art director Dirk Kaufman
U.S. production Chris Avgherinos
U.S. DTP designer Milos Orlovic

This Eyewitness ® Guide has been conceived by
Dorling Kindersley Limited and Editions Gallimard

This edition published in the United States in 2004
by DK Publishing, Inc., 375 Hudson Street, New York, NY 10014

06 07 08 10 9 8 7 6 5 4

Copyright © 1992, © 2004 Dorling Kindersley Limited

A catalog record for this book is
available from the Library of Congress.

ISBN 13: 978-0-7566-0686-2 ISBN 10: 0-7566-0686-1 (PLC)
ISBN 13: 978-0-7566-0685-5 ISBN 10: 0-7566-0685-3 (ALB)

Color reproduction by Colourscan, Singapore
Printed in Hong Kong by Toppan Printing Co.,
(Shenzhen) Ltd.

Archer on horseback,
c. fifth century BCE

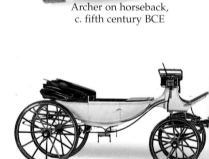

French-style barouche, c. 1880

Discover more at

www.dk.com

Palomino with
Western-style
bridle and saddle

Pair of grays
with English
phaeton, c. 1840

Contents

Pair of Dutch Gelderlanders
pulling covered wagon

The horse family

HORSES, ASSES, AND ZEBRAS all belong to one family of mammals called the Equidae. They are called "odd-toed" animals because they only have one hoof on each foot, while cows and deer have two hooves and are called "even-toed." The Equidae are classified in the order Perissodactyla with their nearest relatives, the rhinoceroses and tapirs. All members of the horse family (equids) feed by grazing on grasses and shrubs, live in open country, and are fast-running animals that depend on speed to escape from predators. All highly social (pp. 12–13), they live in family groups that join together into a herd. They will travel over great distances in search of food or water, or to get away from flies and mosquitoes that plague them in hot weather. Although there is a great variation in size between different breeds of domestic horse (pp. 38–41), they all belong to one species – *Equus caballus*. A pony is defined as a horse that has a height of less than 14.2 hands (58 in/ 148 cm). Various parts of a horse all have different names and are called the "points" of the horse.

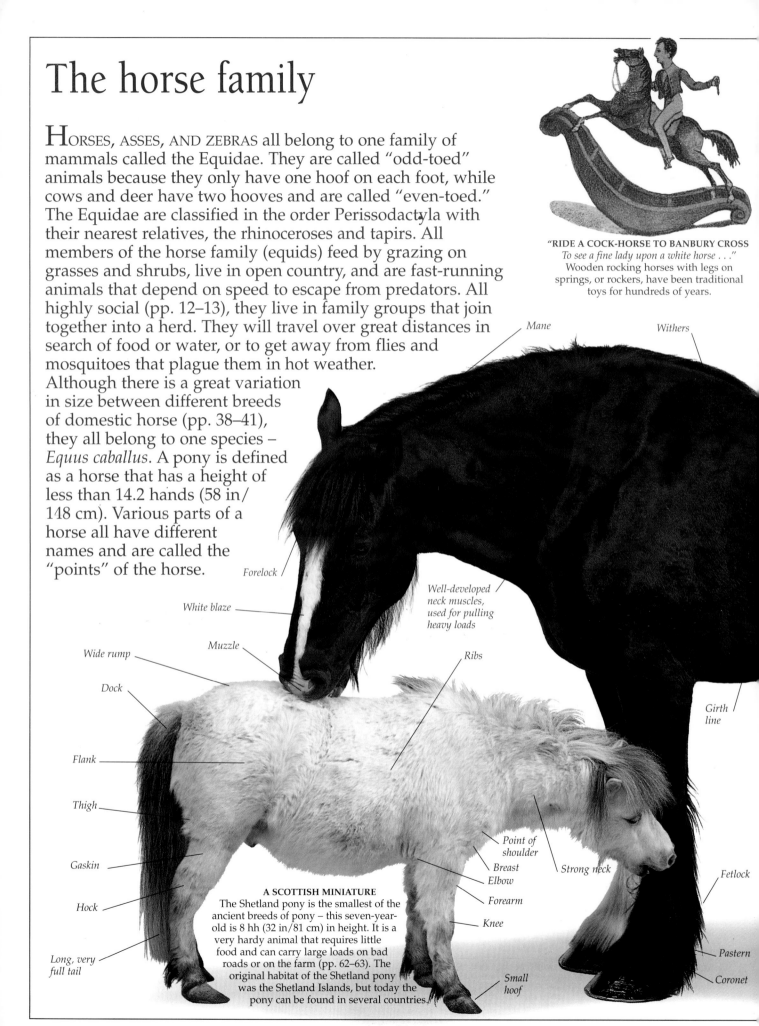

"RIDE A COCK-HORSE TO BANBURY CROSS
To see a fine lady upon a white horse . . ."
Wooden rocking horses with legs on springs, or rockers, have been traditional toys for hundreds of years.

Mane

Withers

Forelock

White blaze

Muzzle

Well-developed neck muscles, used for pulling heavy loads

Ribs

Girth line

Wide rump

Dock

Flank

Thigh

Gaskin

Hock

Long, very full tail

Point of shoulder

Breast

Elbow

Forearm

Knee

Strong neck

Fetlock

Pastern

Coronet

Small hoof

A SCOTTISH MINIATURE
The Shetland pony is the smallest of the ancient breeds of pony – this seven-year-old is 8 hh (32 in/81 cm) in height. It is a very hardy animal that requires little food and can carry large loads on bad roads or on the farm (pp. 62–63). The original habitat of the Shetland pony was the Shetland Islands, but today the pony can be found in several countries.

ASSES AND ZEBRAS
Besides the horse, the other members of the horse family are the Asian wild asses, or onagers (pp. 16–17); the African wild ass (pp. 16–17), which is the ancestor of the domestic donkey (pp. 24–25); and the zebras (pp. 18–19).

No forelock

Heavy head

Dark muzzle

Large ears with dark tips

Short, erect mane

Long, erect ears

Typical white muzzle

Pale brown shadow striping between black stripes

Pale underbelly

Dark muzzle

Kulan – a type of Asian wild ass

Poitou donkey

Common or plains zebra mother and foal

How to measure a horse's height
The height of a horse is measured in hands. One hand, literally the width of an adult's hand, is equal to 4 in (10.16 cm). If a horse measures 15.2 hands, then it is 62 in (157 cm) high. This measurement is taken from its feet to the top of its shoulders, which are called the withers.

Broad back

Very powerful rump

Short tail prevents snagging in harness

A GREAT HORSE
The Shire horse was first bred in the English Midlands for work on farms and for pulling heavy loads (pp. 50–53). This breed is distinguished by its huge size and by the long hair, or "feathering," around the feet. The horse shown here is named King, and he holds the record for the tallest horse in the world. His height at the withers is 19.2 hands (78 in/198 cm).

Feathered feet

Huge hoof

HORNED HEAD
A unicorn is a mythical horse that had a long horn growing out of its forehead. On armor in Medieval times, this "horse" had a lion's tail, two-toed hooves, and a spiraled horn.

EUROPEAN TRAVELERS
Africa has given the world many members of the horse family – from zebras to wild asses. As Europeans explored this vast continent, they brought their domesticated horses with them to use as transportation. This elaborate wood carving of human and animal figures (including horses) was made by Ibo people in Nigeria, West Africa.

How horses evolved

IT TOOK ABOUT 55 MILLION YEARS for the present family of horses, asses, and zebras (equids) to evolve (gradually change) from their earliest horselike ancestor. Originally called *Eohippus*, or "dawn horse" – because it lived during the Eocene epoch – it is now known as *Hyracotherium*. This early horse was not much larger than a hare. It was a "browsing" animal – which fed on leaves and shrubs – and had four hoofed toes on its front feet and three on its hind feet. It lived in the woodlands of Europe, North America, and eastern Asia. Gradually, over millions of years, this small animal evolved into a "grazing" (grass-eating) mammal with three hoofed toes, and later, with a single hoof, on all feet. At first, browsing horses, like *Mesohippus* and then *Parahippus*, had low-crowned teeth (pp. 10–11), but during the later Miocene epoch (20 million years ago) grasslands began to replace the woodlands in North America. In adapting to this new environment, ancestral horses evolved longer limbs that enabled them to range over a wide area in search of pasture and to escape from predators. At the same time, their teeth became high-crowned in order to adapt to their diet of tough grasses. The first grazing horse was *Merychippus*, but eventually it was replaced by *Pliohippus*, the first one-toed horse. This gave rise to *Equus* during the Pleistocene (about two million years ago).

Side toe

Hoof of side toe

Main hoof core

Side view of left hind foot of *Hipparion*

Left side toe

Right side hoof

Hoof of small side toe

Main hoof core

Front view of hind foot of *Hipparion*

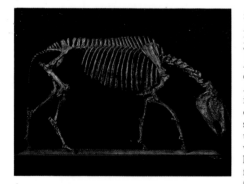

Nasal bone

Incisor tooth

SOUTH AMERICAN HORSE
This is the skeleton of *Hippidion*, an extinct one-toed equid that evolved in Central America and then spread into South America. Its descendant, *Onohippidium*, survived in South America until at least 12,000 years ago, when their extinction may have been hastened by the first human hunters moving through the continent at the end of the Ice Age.

Ear bone

Orbit, or eye socket

LAST OF THE THREE-TOED HORSES
Hipparion (side view of skull, above) was the last of the three-toed equids. It was a very successful grazer with high-crowned teeth, and its fossil remains have been found in many parts of Europe, Asia, and Africa. *Hipparion* did not finally become extinct in Africa until about 125,000 years ago.

Incisor for cutting food

Lost incisor

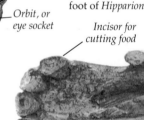

Four-toed

Three-toed

Three-toed

Three-toed

One-toed

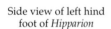

Hyracotherium

Mesohippus

Parahippus

Merychippus

Pliohippus

BROWSERS

GRAZERS

EQUINE SIDELINE
The three-toed fossil horse *Anchitherium* was very successful and spread from America through Asia and Europe in the early Miocene epoch (about 24 million years ago). However, it was an equine sideline – that is, one that did not evolve into the modern horse. It became extinct before the beginning of the Pliocene epoch, about five million years ago.

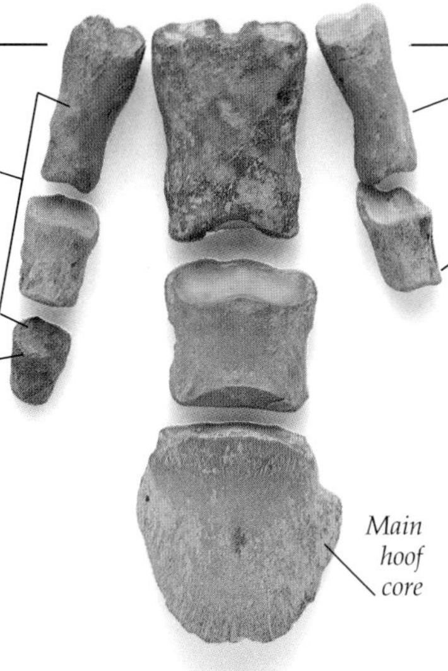

Side toe

Side toe – hoof core missing

Side hoof core

Main hoof core

Lower cheek teeth (molars and premolars)

Foot and toe bones of *Anchitherium*

Upper cheek teeth

Upper jaw of *Anchitherium*

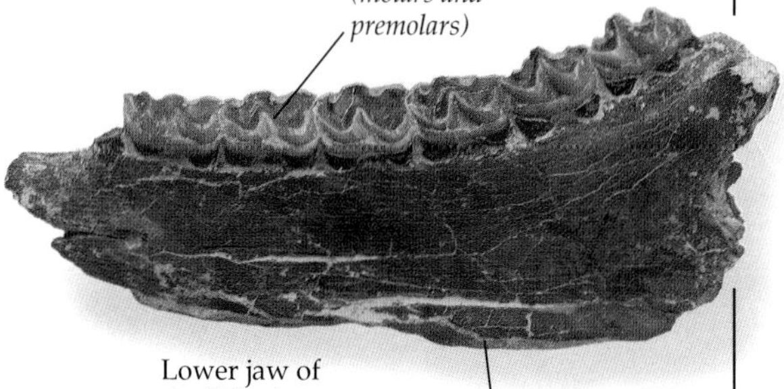

Lower jaw of *Anchitherium*

Part of mandible (jaw bone)

Parietal bone

THE OLDEST EQUID
The palatal (roof of mouth) view of the skull of a fossil *Hyracotherium* from the Eocene epoch (54 million years ago) in England shows the square, six-lobed teeth that were the foundation from which the teeth of modern horses evolved.

Orbit, or eye socket

Palatal bone

Cranium for brain

Ear bone

Base of skull

Palatal view of *Hyracotherium* skull, showing roof of mouth

Orbit

Nasal bone

Cheek teeth

Side view of right half of *Hyracotherium* skull

High-crowned teeth used for chewing

Orbit

Foramen magnum (hole for spinal cord)

Base of cranium

Ear bone

Palatal view of *Hipparion* skull

One-toed

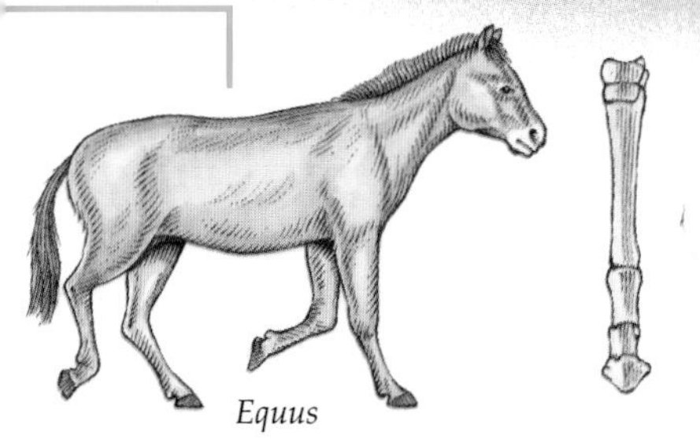

Equus

GRAZERS

FIRST THREE-TOED HORSE
Mesohippus, which lived during the Oligocene epoch about 37 million years ago, was the first horse to have three toes (with the middle toe larger than the two side ones) and was the same size as a sheep.

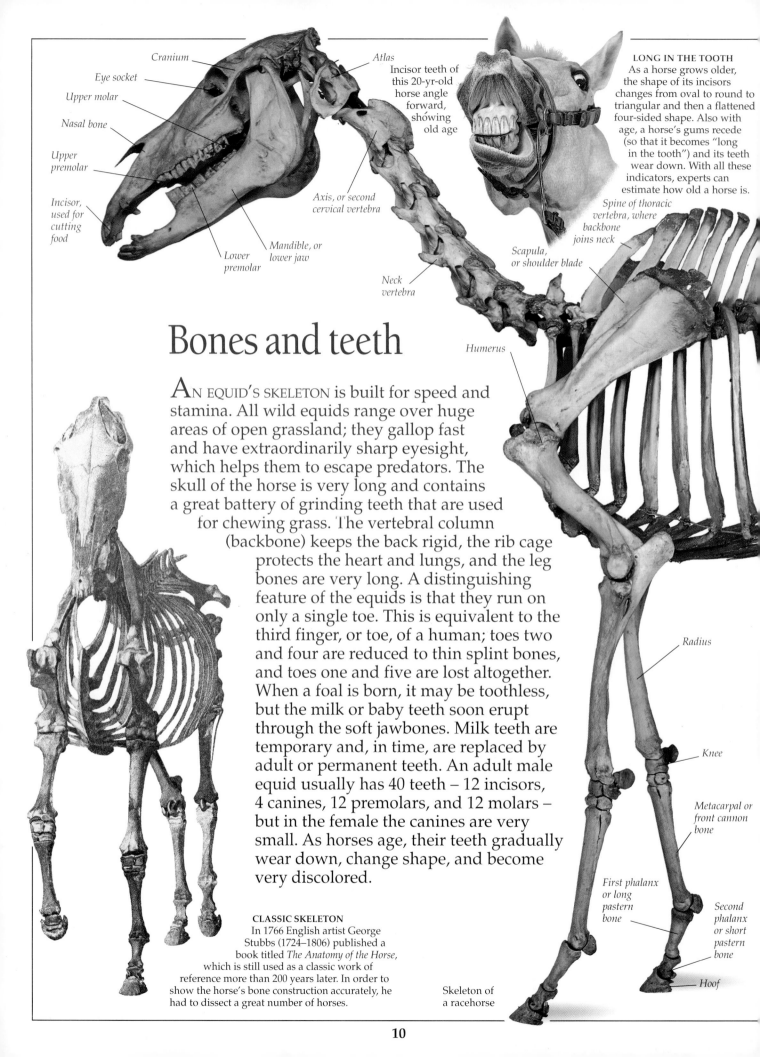

Cranium

Eye socket

Upper molar

Nasal bone

Upper premolar

Incisor, used for cutting food

Lower premolar

Mandible, or lower jaw

Atlas

Incisor teeth of this 20-yr-old horse angle forward, showing old age

Axis, or second cervical vertebra

Neck vertebra

LONG IN THE TOOTH
As a horse grows older, the shape of its incisors changes from oval to round to triangular and then a flattened four-sided shape. Also with age, a horse's gums recede (so that it becomes "long in the tooth") and its teeth wear down. With all these indicators, experts can estimate how old a horse is.

Spine of thoracic vertebra, where backbone joins neck

Scapula, or shoulder blade

Humerus

Bones and teeth

AN EQUID'S SKELETON is built for speed and stamina. All wild equids range over huge areas of open grassland; they gallop fast and have extraordinarily sharp eyesight, which helps them to escape predators. The skull of the horse is very long and contains a great battery of grinding teeth that are used for chewing grass. The vertebral column (backbone) keeps the back rigid, the rib cage protects the heart and lungs, and the leg bones are very long. A distinguishing feature of the equids is that they run on only a single toe. This is equivalent to the third finger, or toe, of a human; toes two and four are reduced to thin splint bones, and toes one and five are lost altogether. When a foal is born, it may be toothless, but the milk or baby teeth soon erupt through the soft jawbones. Milk teeth are temporary and, in time, are replaced by adult or permanent teeth. An adult male equid usually has 40 teeth – 12 incisors, 4 canines, 12 premolars, and 12 molars – but in the female the canines are very small. As horses age, their teeth gradually wear down, change shape, and become very discolored.

Radius

Knee

Metacarpal or front cannon bone

First phalanx or long pastern bone

Second phalanx or short pastern bone

Hoof

CLASSIC SKELETON
In 1766 English artist George Stubbs (1724–1806) published a book titled *The Anatomy of the Horse*, which is still used as a classic work of reference more than 200 years later. In order to show the horse's bone construction accurately, he had to dissect a great number of horses.

Skeleton of a racehorse

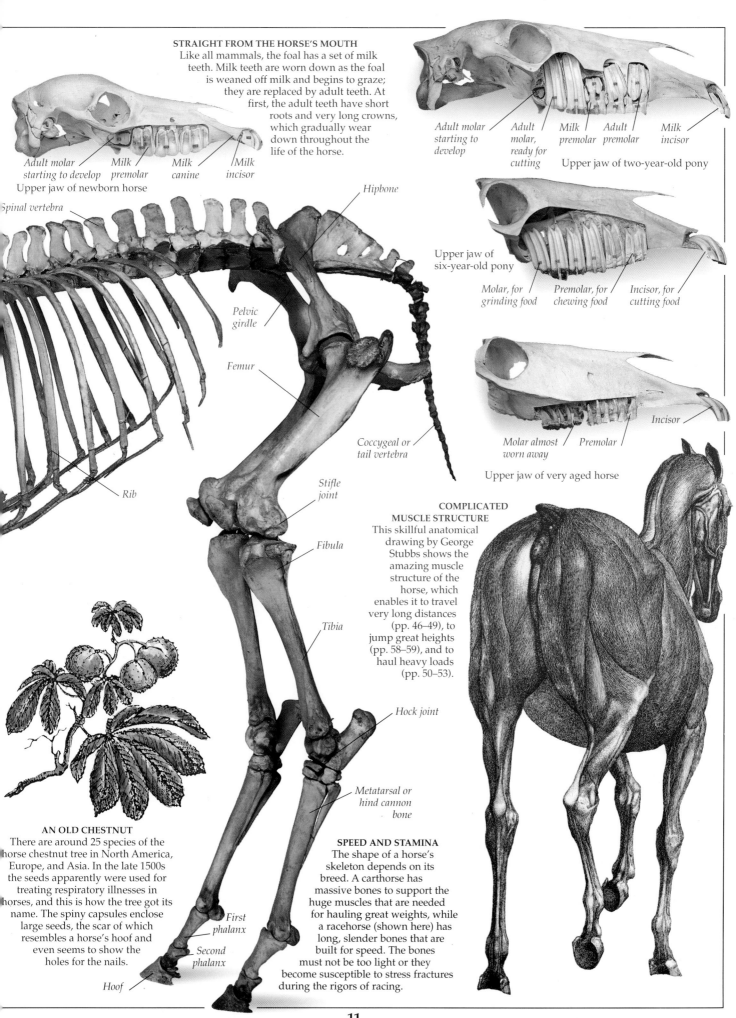

STRAIGHT FROM THE HORSE'S MOUTH
Like all mammals, the foal has a set of milk teeth. Milk teeth are worn down as the foal is weaned off milk and begins to graze; they are replaced by adult teeth. At first, the adult teeth have short roots and very long crowns, which gradually wear down throughout the life of the horse.

Adult molar starting to develop *Milk premolar* *Milk canine* *Milk incisor*

Upper jaw of newborn horse

Adult molar starting to develop *Adult molar, ready for cutting* *Milk premolar* *Adult premolar* *Milk incisor*

Upper jaw of two-year-old pony

Upper jaw of six-year-old pony

Molar, for grinding food *Premolar, for chewing food* *Incisor, for cutting food*

Molar almost worn away *Premolar* *Incisor*

Upper jaw of very aged horse

Spinal vertebra

Hipbone

Pelvic girdle

Femur

Coccygeal or tail vertebra

Rib

Stifle joint

Fibula

Tibia

Hock joint

COMPLICATED MUSCLE STRUCTURE
This skillful anatomical drawing by George Stubbs shows the amazing muscle structure of the horse, which enables it to travel very long distances (pp. 46–49), to jump great heights (pp. 58–59), and to haul heavy loads (pp. 50–53).

Metatarsal or hind cannon bone

AN OLD CHESTNUT
There are around 25 species of the horse chestnut tree in North America, Europe, and Asia. In the late 1500s the seeds apparently were used for treating respiratory illnesses in horses, and this is how the tree got its name. The spiny capsules enclose large seeds, the scar of which resembles a horse's hoof and even seems to show the holes for the nails.

First phalanx

Second phalanx

Hoof

SPEED AND STAMINA
The shape of a horse's skeleton depends on its breed. A carthorse has massive bones to support the huge muscles that are needed for hauling great weights, while a racehorse (shown here) has long, slender bones that are built for speed. The bones must not be too light or they become susceptible to stress fractures during the rigors of racing.

11

Senses and behavior

Ears pointing back show anger or fear

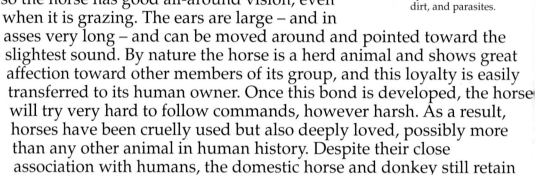

ROLLING OVER
This pony is having a good roll, which is an important part of grooming. It relaxes the muscles and helps to remove loose hair, dirt, and parasites.

HORSES, ASSES, AND ZEBRAS all have more highly developed senses of sight, hearing, and smell than humans. The characteristic long face of the horse holds not only the large teeth but also the sensitive organs of smell. The eyes are set far up in the skull and are positioned on the sides of the head, so the horse has good all-around vision, even when it is grazing. The ears are large – and in asses very long – and can be moved around and pointed toward the slightest sound. By nature the horse is a herd animal and shows great affection toward other members of its group, and this loyalty is easily transferred to its human owner. Once this bond is developed, the horse will try very hard to follow commands, however harsh. As a result, horses have been cruelly used but also deeply loved, possibly more than any other animal in human history. Despite their close association with humans, the domestic horse and donkey still retain the instincts and natural behavioral patterns of their wild ancestors. They will defend their territory and suckle their foals in just the same way as will the wild horse and the wild ass, and they will always need companionship.

Ears pointing forward show interest in surroundings

One ear forward, one ear back shows uncertainty

TWO-WAY STRETCH
An equid's ears have a dual role – to pick up sounds and to transmit visual signals. If a mule (shown here) lays its ears back, it is frightened or angry. If they are forward, then it is interested in what is happening around it, such as the clatter of a food bucket. One ear forward and one back means it is not sure what will happen next.

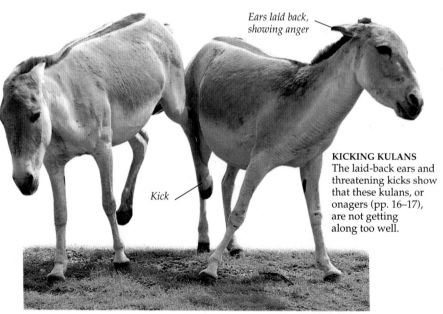

Ears laid back, showing anger

Kick

KICKING KULANS
The laid-back ears and threatening kicks show that these kulans, or onagers (pp. 16–17), are not getting along too well.

Zebra calling, to warn other animals in the herd of danger

PROTECTING TERRITORY AND FAMILY
Fighting by rearing and stabbing with their front hooves is natural to all equids. However, they may prefer to settle their differences by threats with their ears, tails, and feet and by using other body language. Stallions and geldings (sterilized males) will fight over territory or to protect their mares, as shown by these Icelandic ponies.

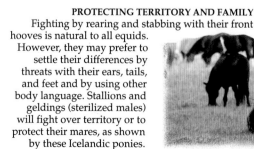

Cartoon shows lead horse ignoring his driver's commands and taking the liberty of stopping for a drink

FLEHMEN REACTION
By pulling back his lips and drawing air in over his vomeronasal, or Jacobson's, organ after smelling a mare's urine, this stallion is testing whether she is ready to mate – that is, whether she is in heat ("in estrus"). This is called the flehmen reaction.

Bite given to unfamiliar horse

A BITE THREAT
These horses, from two different herds, are trying to show who is more important, or "dominant," with one horse showing a bite threat to the other. The attacking horse's neck is thrust forward and it is trying to bite its opponent.

THE BEST OF FRIENDS
Two horses will often stand close together, head to tail, nuzzling each other's manes and backs, thus establishing their relationship. The frequency of these grooming and cleaning sessions varies from season to season, but they usually last around three minutes.

Ears laid back showing shock of bite attack

13

Mares and foals

A MARE, OR FEMALE HORSE, ASS, OR ZEBRA usually gives birth to one foal after a gestation period, or carrying time, of 11 months or a little longer. The mares mate with a stallion in spring; all the foals are then born the following spring when there is fresh grass. The gestation period is as long as a year because the mother must produce a healthy, well-developed foal (or very rarely twins); the foal can walk within an hour after birth and can soon keep up with the moving herd. Although the mare will continue to suckle her foal for up to a year, the foal begins to graze after a few weeks. Asses (pp. 16–17), zebras (pp. 18–19), and horses are all grazers that live on open grasslands where food can be scarce, and young animals could be an easy target for large predators, such as lions in Africa. Between the ages of one and four years, a female foal is called a filly and a male foal a colt. In the wild, fillies and colts leave their mothers' herds and form new groups of their own when they mature.

A PREGNANT PALOMINO
This Palomino (pp. 38–39) shows by her large belly that she will soon give birth. Both feral and domestic mares (pp. 36–37) tend to give birth quickly, but highly bred horses are usually carefully watched in case something goes wrong.

A NEWBORN FOAL
This mare is resting for a few minutes after giving birth to her foal, which still has part of the amniotic or birth sac over its back. Soon the foal will kick free from its mother, breaking off the umbilical cord, which has provided it with nourishment up to now in the uterus (womb).

LICKING INTO SHAPE
The mare gets to her feet and removes the birth sac by licking the foal all over. This also helps strengthen the foal's circulation and breathing.

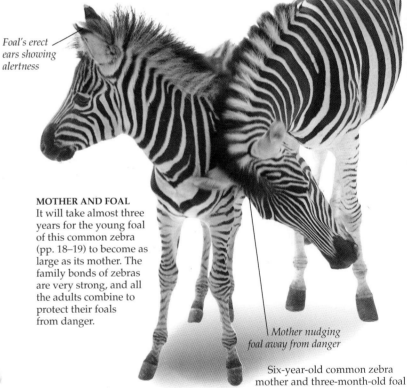

Foal's erect ears showing alertness

MOTHER AND FOAL
It will take almost three years for the young foal of this common zebra (pp. 18–19) to become as large as its mother. The family bonds of zebras are very strong, and all the adults combine to protect their foals from danger.

Mother nudging foal away from danger

Six-year-old common zebra mother and three-month-old foal

THE FIRST DRINK
As soon as it can stand, the foal will search for the mother's teats between her hind legs and will begin to suck. The first milk is called colostrum, and it helps the foal build up lifelong immunity to disease.

STANDING ON ITS OWN FOUR FEET
While the mother looks around for danger, the foal takes its first faltering steps.

WATCH OUT!
Although this Shire mare (pp. 50–53) is descended from horses that have been domesticated for thousands of years (pp. 22–23), she still has the instincts of her wild ancestors and will be constantly on guard against possible danger to her foal.

Alert ears listening for signs of danger

KEEPING UP
A foal is on its feet within an hour of birth, and it must try to keep up with its mother – particularly in the wild.

Height at withers 17.3 hands (71 in/ 180 cm)

Mother's muzzle protecting foal

Height at withers 11.2 hands (46 in/117 cm)

Ten-year-old Shire mother and her five-week-old foal

. . . AND SO TO BED
Like all babies, a foal needs a great deal of rest, but it can get to its feet very quickly if danger threatens.

15

Wild asses

THERE ARE THREE SPECIES of wild ass, and they are no more closely related to one another than the horse is to the zebra. They can interbreed, but their offspring will be infertile (pp. 18–19). The three species are the true wild ass of Africa (*Equus africanus*), which until recently ranged over the Sahara Desert in North Africa, and the two species of Asian wild asses – the onager (*Equus hemionus*) from the Middle East and northwest India, and the kiang (*Equus kiang*) from the Tibetan plateau, north of the Himalayas. Of these three species, it is the African wild ass that is the ancestor of the domestic donkey (pp. 24–25). All wild asses look similar – a heavy head, long ears, a short mane, no forelock, slender legs, and a wispy tail. The African wild ass is grayish in color, with a white belly and a dark stripe along its back; it often has horizontal stripes around its legs and a black stripe over its shoulders. The Asian wild asses are redder in color and never have leg or shoulder stripes, though they do have a dark line along the back. All wild asses are adapted for life in the arid, rocky environment of the semideserts and mountain plateaus of Africa and Asia, where they graze on thornbushes and dry grass. Today, all wild asses are in danger of extinction from loss of their habitat and overhunting by humans.

FIRST CATCH YOUR ONAGER
The above scenes of catching wild onagers alive (c. 645 B.C.) are from the stone friezes that adorned the palace of Nineveh in Assyria. These Syrian onagers (now extinct) were perhaps being caught for crossbreeding (pp. 26–27) with domestic donkeys or horses

Long, wispy tail

PRESERVATION
Until recently, there were several races of African wild asses. The Somali wild ass (*Equus africanus somaliensis*), the only African ass still to survive in the wild, usually has stripes around its legs, but not on its shoulders. These asses have been taken to a wildlife reserve in Israel to try to save the species, whose home is in Ethiopia and Somalia.

Slender, pale-colored leg

NOW EXTINCT
The Nubian wild ass (*Equus africanus africanus*) is now extinct. It differed from the Somali ass in that it had a very short, dark stripe across its shoulders but no horizontal stripes on its legs.

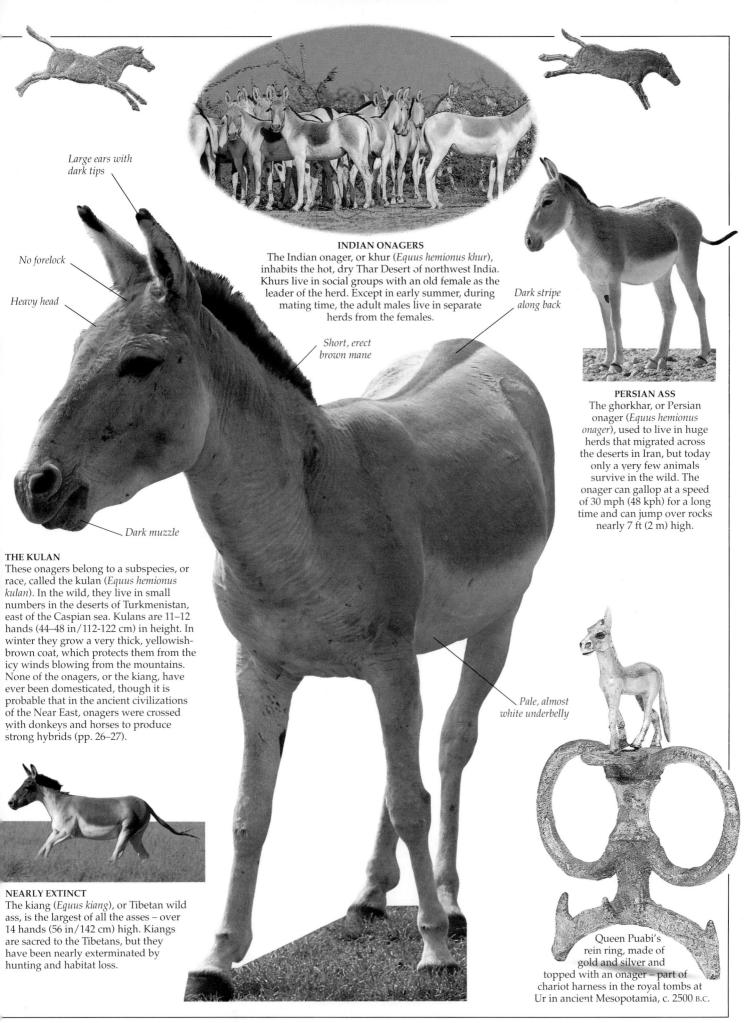

Large ears with dark tips

No forelock

Heavy head

INDIAN ONAGERS
The Indian onager, or khur (*Equus hemionus khur*), inhabits the hot, dry Thar Desert of northwest India. Khurs live in social groups with an old female as the leader of the herd. Except in early summer, during mating time, the adult males live in separate herds from the females.

Short, erect brown mane

Dark stripe along back

Dark muzzle

PERSIAN ASS
The ghorkhar, or Persian onager (*Equus hemionus onager*), used to live in huge herds that migrated across the deserts in Iran, but today only a very few animals survive in the wild. The onager can gallop at a speed of 30 mph (48 kph) for a long time and can jump over rocks nearly 7 ft (2 m) high.

THE KULAN
These onagers belong to a subspecies, or race, called the kulan (*Equus hemionus kulan*). In the wild, they live in small numbers in the deserts of Turkmenistan, east of the Caspian sea. Kulans are 11–12 hands (44–48 in/112-122 cm) in height. In winter they grow a very thick, yellowish-brown coat, which protects them from the icy winds blowing from the mountains. None of the onagers, or the kiang, have ever been domesticated, though it is probable that in the ancient civilizations of the Near East, onagers were crossed with donkeys and horses to produce strong hybrids (pp. 26–27).

Pale, almost white underbelly

NEARLY EXTINCT
The kiang (*Equus kiang*), or Tibetan wild ass, is the largest of all the asses – over 14 hands (56 in/142 cm) high. Kiangs are sacred to the Tibetans, but they have been nearly exterminated by hunting and habitat loss.

Queen Puabi's rein ring, made of gold and silver and topped with an onager – part of chariot harness in the royal tombs at Ur in ancient Mesopotamia, c. 2500 B.C.

Seeing stripes

Today, zebras live only in Africa, although their ancestors, like all other members of the horse family, evolved in North America. There are three living species of zebra – Grevy's, common, and mountain – each found in different habitats and having different patterns of stripes. Sharply defined stripes are seen only on short-coated animals in the tropics. The quagga, a fourth species that used to live in the colder climate of Africa's southern tip but was exterminated by hunters by the late 1800s, had a thicker coat and fewer stripes on its body. Zebras feed on coarse grasses and move over huge areas as they graze. They are very social and spend much time grooming, nuzzling each other's manes and withers with their front teeth. Zebras live in family groups, in herds of a hundred or more. It is not known why zebras are striped, but it is not for camouflage since they never hide from predators such as lions or hyenas. Instead, zebras will stand tightly together and defend themselves with their hooves and teeth.

Large, rounded ears

BIG EARS
The Grévy's large, round ears are used to signal other individuals as well as to listen for sounds over great distances in its semidesert habitat.

Oval ears

Very dark muzzle

Small, squarish dewlap on throat

No stripes on belly

Thinner stripes down legs

Seven-year-old female mountain zebra

MOUNTAIN ZEBRA
The mountain zebra (*Equus zebra*) is now an endangered species that may soon be extinct like the quagga. It is found in small numbers in the mountain ranges of the western Cape province of South Africa and up the west coast to Angola. Like the common zebra, the mountain zebra averages around 13 hands (52 in/132 cm) at the withers.

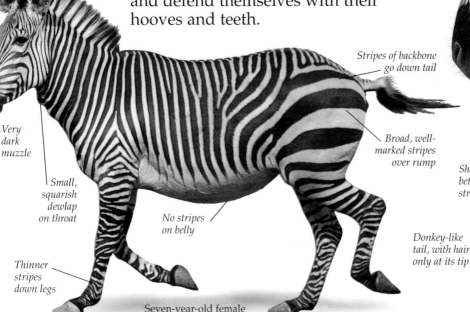

White ears with black tips

Stripes of backbone go down tail

Broad, well-marked stripes over rump

Shadows between stripes

Donkey-like tail, with hair only at its tip

Six-year-old common or plains zebra mare and her three-month-old foal

ZEBROID
Zebras can interbreed with all other horse species, but their offspring are infertile, like that of the mule (pp. 26–27). The animal shown left is a zorse, a cross (hybrid) between a zebra and a horse.

COMMON STRIPES
The common zebra (*Equus burchelli*), at around 13 hands (52 in/132 cm), once ranged throughout eastern and southern Africa, from Sudan to the Cape. Today, it is still widespread, and herds can be seen in almost all wildlife reserves. Young males live in bachelor groups until they can form their own families. Zebras are very social – if one member of the group is missing, they will search for it.

Dorsal or back stripe is broad and black

Very narrow stripes on face

GRÉVY'S ZEBRA
Grévy's zebra (*Equus grevyi*) is the most northern of the species and lives in small numbers in the semidesert areas of Kenya, Ethiopia, and Somalia. It is the largest of the zebras, with an average height of 14–15 hands (56–60 in/142–152 cm). It is not closely related to the other zebras and is considered to be a more primitive member of the horse family.

Rounded ears

No forelock

V-shaped brown patch on nose

Very tall, erect mane

White on either side of black dorsal stripe

Narrow, closely spaced black stripes on a white background, especially over the withers

White underbelly

Two female Grévy's zebras, age three to four years

Pale-brown shadow striping between black stripes

Broad hooves

Stripes go down legs, ending in black coronet, above hoof

Black dorsal stripe becomes thinner down the tail, with stripes on either side

Stripes bend around, becoming horizontal over haunches

White inside of leg with no stripes

THE HORSE-LIKE QUAGGA
Early explorers in southern Africa found herds of more than 100 quaggas (*Equus quagga*) on their yearly migrations to different grazing grounds. Gradually, they were reduced in numbers by indiscriminate hunting; the last wild quaggas were shot in 1861. Efforts are now being made to recreate the quagga by selectively breeding plains zebras.

ZEDONK
Another type of crossbreeding – between a zebra and a donkey – can result in pale-brown-colored animals with very fine stripes, such as these zedonks from Zimbabwe in south-central Africa. Many zoos around the world carry out successful crossbreeding programs.

Ancient ancestors

Fossil evidence tells us that at the end of the last ice age, 10,000 years ago (pp. 8–9), there must have been millions of horses living wild all over Europe and in northern and central Asia. These animals belonged to one species, called *Equus ferus*, that roamed in herds over the grasslands and probably migrated for hundreds of miles each year. As the climate changed, the grasslands were replaced by forests. The horses dwindled in number from loss of their habitat (area in which they lived) and from extensive hunting by humans. By 4,000 years ago very few wild horses were left in Europe, though two sub-species of wild horse – in Russia, the tarpan (*Equus ferus ferus*), and in Mongolia, Przewalski's horse (*Equus ferus przewalskii*) – survived until relatively recently. Also around 4,000 years ago, the first wild horses were being tamed and domesticated in eastern Europe, and they soon spread westward (pp. 22–23). All the domestic horses in the world today are descended from these domesticated ancestors, and they are classified in one species, called *Equus caballus*.

EXTINCT WILD HORSE
Many 18th-century travelers to the Russian steppes (plains) described herds of small wild horses, some of which were probably feral (pp. 32–33). The last tarpans died out in the early 1800s. In Poland today, ponies very like the tarpan have been re-created by breeding from primitive breeds such as the Konik.

Height range at withers of 13–14 hands (52–56 in/ 132–142 cm)

Short mane

Short forelock

AN ANCIENT ENGLISH PONY
The Exmoor pony is an ancient breed that closely resembles the extinct tarpan, or wild pony of eastern Europe. These ponies live in feral herds at Exmoor in southwest England.

Light-colored, flecked muzzle, typical of wild horse

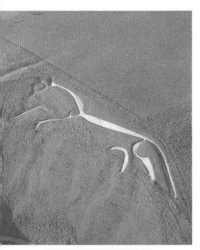

SACRED WHITE HORSE
White horses were sacred animals to the Celts who lived in western Europe around 500 B.C. Around that time, this impression of a horse was scraped out from the white chalk hills at Whitehorse Hill in Berkshire, southern England.

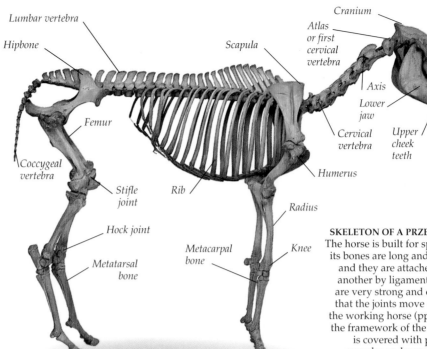

Lumbar vertebra
Hipbone
Femur
Coccygeal vertebra
Stifle joint
Hock joint
Metatarsal bone
Rib
Scapula
Cranium
Atlas or first cervical vertebra
Eye socket
Nasal bone
Axis
Lower jaw
Cervical vertebra
Upper cheek teeth
Humerus
Radius
Metacarpal bone
Knee

SKELETON OF A PRZEWALSKI
The horse is built for speed. All its bones are long and slender, and they are attached to one another by ligaments, which are very strong and elastic so that the joints move easily. In the working horse (pp. 50–53), the framework of the skeleton is covered with powerful muscles and very little fat.

PRZEWALSKI HORSES
Wild horses were found living on the steppes of Mongolia by Russian travelers in the 1880s. A few were brought to Europe, where they bred in zoos and were later taken to America. Przewalski horses have been extinct in the wild since the 1960s, but now they are being reintroduced to Mongolia from herds bred in captivity.

Long, shaggy tail

Group of Przewalski horses

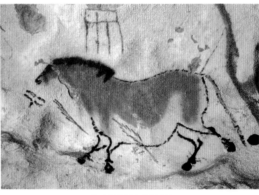

CAVE PAINTINGS
This wild horse (*Equus ferus*) was painted on a wall in the famous caves at Lascaux, France, by hunting people toward the end of the last ice age, about 14,000 years ago.

WILD AFRICAN ASS
The African wild ass (*Equus africanus*) is the ancestor of all domestic donkeys (pp. 24–25). It is still found in very small numbers in the eastern Sahara, but it is in danger of extinction.

Horses in history

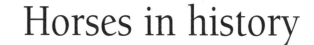

THE EARLIEST RELIABLE EVIDENCE for the domesticati of the horse comes from the Ukraine, where people lived by herding horses and cattle on the grass steppes 6,000 years ago. At the same time, the African wild ass (pp. 16–17) was being domesticated in ancient Egypt and Arabia. At first horses and asses were not usually ridden, but were harnessed in a pair to a ca or chariot. Soon chariots became the status symbols of kings, who rode in them to battle, in royal parades, and for hunting. By the time of Home the eighth-century-B.C. Greek poet, the riding of horses and donkeys had become a common means of travel (pp. 46–49), but chariots were still used for warfar (pp. 42–45). In the classical period of civilization, the ancier Greeks and Romans built special arenas and tracks for chariot races, which provided high drama for the crowds who watched these sporting events, involving riders, drive and horses (pp. 59–61).

THE END OF THE DAY
This horse's head from the Parthenon marbles (5th century B.C.) in Athens, Greece, is one of the greatest sculptures of all time. Legend has it that a team of horses would pull the Sun's chariot to the sea each day to create the sunset. The exhaustion from this extreme effort shows on the horse's face.

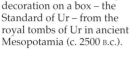

ROYAL STANDARD
This very early representation of donkeys harnessed to a four-wheeled cart is part of the mosaic decoration on a box – the Standard of Ur – from the royal tombs of Ur in ancient Mesopotamia (c. 2500 B.C.).

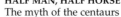

FLYING THROUGH THE AIR
Pegasus was a mythical horse with wings, who according to the ancient Greeks had sprung from the blood of Medusa when Perseus, a son of Zeus, cut off her head. The horse flew up to join the gods, but he was caught by Athena, the goddess of wisdom, and tamed with a golden bridle. This exquisite engraving of Pegasus is on a bronze cista, a container used to carry sacred utensils, made by the Etruscans, c. 300 B.C.

READY FOR WAR
This terra-cotta model from Cyprus probably represents an Assyrian warrior, 7th century B.C. The man carries a shield and is ready for battle. His horse has a breastplate and a warlike headdress.

HALF MAN, HALF HORSE
The myth of the centaurs – half men, half horses – may have arisen when people in ancient Greece saw the horsemen of Thessaly. Because they were unfamiliar with men on horseback, they believed they were seeing a new form of being. Shown here is a scene from the epic battles between the wild and lawless centaurs and the Lapiths of northern Greece which appears in the sculptures in the Parthenon, fifth century B.C.

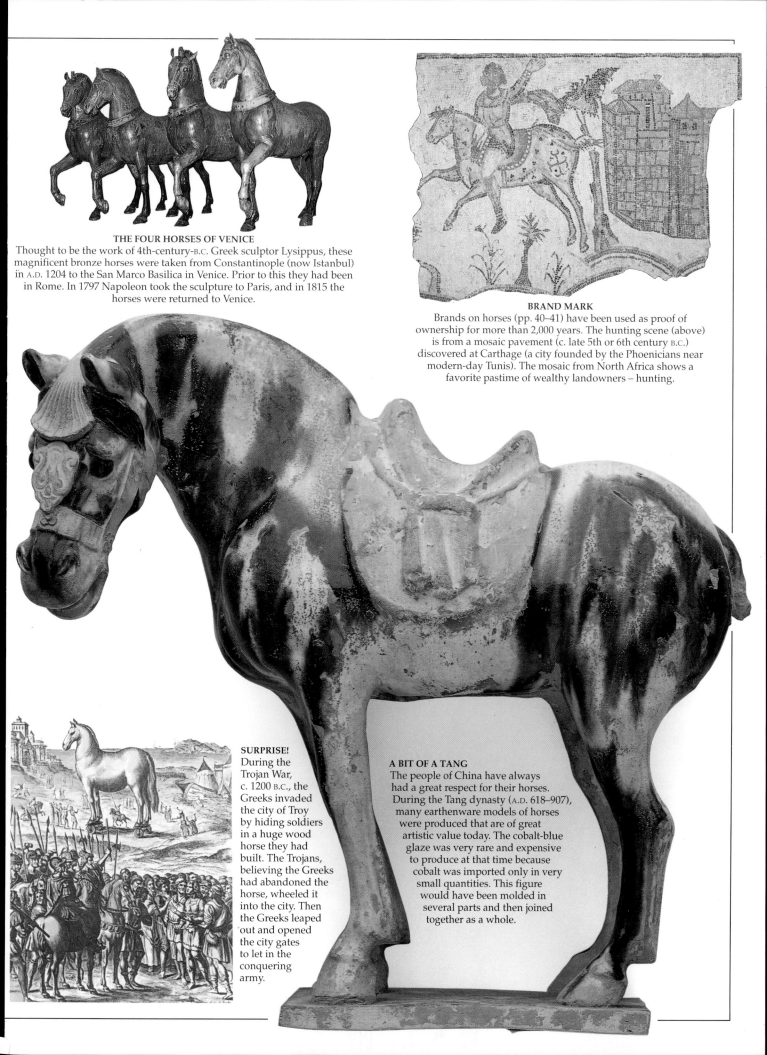

THE FOUR HORSES OF VENICE
Thought to be the work of 4th-century-B.C. Greek sculptor Lysippus, these magnificent bronze horses were taken from Constantinople (now Istanbul) in A.D. 1204 to the San Marco Basilica in Venice. Prior to this they had been in Rome. In 1797 Napoleon took the sculpture to Paris, and in 1815 the horses were returned to Venice.

BRAND MARK
Brands on horses (pp. 40–41) have been used as proof of ownership for more than 2,000 years. The hunting scene (above) is from a mosaic pavement (c. late 5th or 6th century B.C.) discovered at Carthage (a city founded by the Phoenicians near modern-day Tunis). The mosaic from North Africa shows a favorite pastime of wealthy landowners – hunting.

SURPRISE!
During the Trojan War, c. 1200 B.C., the Greeks invaded the city of Troy by hiding soldiers in a huge wood horse they had built. The Trojans, believing the Greeks had abandoned the horse, wheeled it into the city. Then the Greeks leaped out and opened the city gates to let in the conquering army.

A BIT OF A TANG
The people of China have always had a great respect for their horses. During the Tang dynasty (A.D. 618–907), many earthenware models of horses were produced that are of great artistic value today. The cobalt-blue glaze was very rare and expensive to produce at that time because cobalt was imported only in very small quantities. This figure would have been molded in several parts and then joined together as a whole.

Donkey work

T HE DOMESTICATED ASS, OR DONKEY (*Equus asinus*), is descended from the African wild ass (*Equus africanus*, pp. 16–17), which lives in the hot, dry deserts of the Sahara and Arabia. Because of this harsh environment, the donkey has developed great strength, stamina, and endurance to carry heavy loads over long distances on little food and water. In the wild, donkey foals have to develop quickly so that they can keep up with the herd as it travels great distances in search of edible bushes and grass. Female donkeys, or jennies, carry their foals for 12 months before they are born – a gestation period of two months more than the female horse (pp. 14–15). In the desert and on stony ground the donkey's small, neat hooves are kept evenly worn down, but they will grow and must be filed if the animal is kept on soft grass. Like all members of the horse family, the donkey is a social animal and needs to live with other animals if it is to thrive.

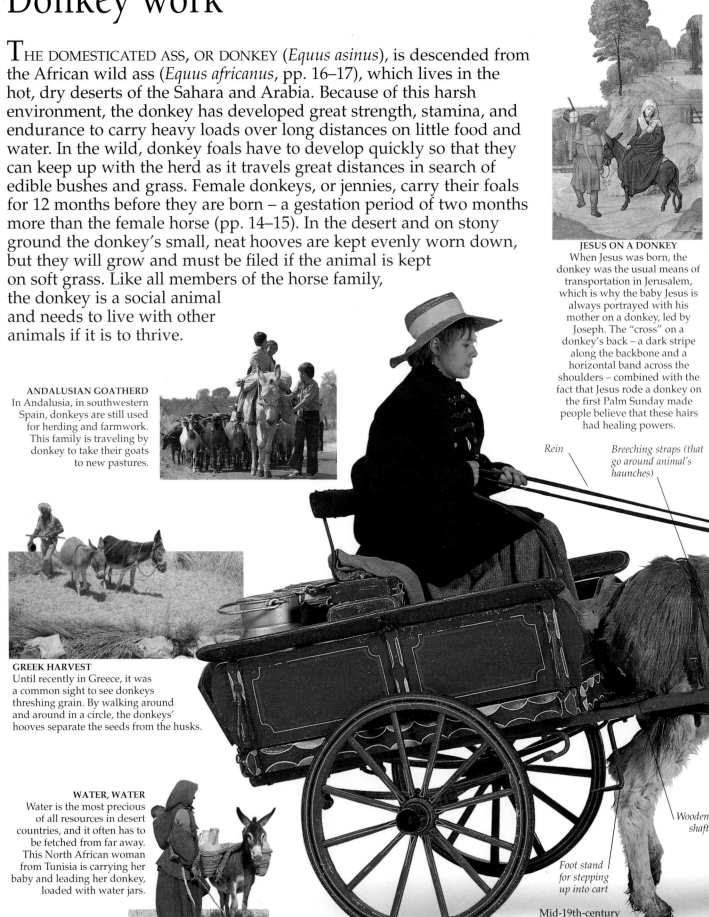

JESUS ON A DONKEY
When Jesus was born, the donkey was the usual means of transportation in Jerusalem, which is why the baby Jesus is always portrayed with his mother on a donkey, led by Joseph. The "cross" on a donkey's back – a dark stripe along the backbone and a horizontal band across the shoulders – combined with the fact that Jesus rode a donkey on the first Palm Sunday made people believe that these hairs had healing powers.

ANDALUSIAN GOATHERD
In Andalusia, in southwestern Spain, donkeys are still used for herding and farmwork. This family is traveling by donkey to take their goats to new pastures.

GREEK HARVEST
Until recently in Greece, it was a common sight to see donkeys threshing grain. By walking around and around in a circle, the donkeys' hooves separate the seeds from the husks.

WATER, WATER
Water is the most precious of all resources in desert countries, and it often has to be fetched from far away. This North African woman from Tunisia is carrying her baby and leading her donkey, loaded with water jars.

Rein

Breeching straps (that go around animal's haunches)

Wooden shaft

Foot stand for stepping up into cart

Mid-19th-century English donkey cart

Long ears help donkey keep cool

Lighter baby or juvenile coat on back

Darker adult coat, like his father's, now visible at first shedding

Typical white muzzle

POITOU DONKEYS
For hundreds of years in Spain and in the Poitou region of France, there has been a tradition of breeding very large donkeys, which are used to mate with female horses to produce giant mules (pp. 26–27) for farmwork, in the same way cart horses were used in more northern countries. Poitou donkeys stand about 14 hands (56 in/ 142 cm) at the shoulder, or withers, making them the world's largest donkeys. They also have very long, dark, shaggy coats.

White underbelly

A family group: five-year-old father, nine-year-old mother, and eleven-month-old son

Long, slender legs

This poor old donkey has had a hard working life and now deserves a peaceful retirement

Terret

Rein ring

Bridle

Decorated browband

Blinker

Noseband

Bit

Collar

Trace

Girth

Ten-year-old Irish donkey, at 11.2 hands (46 in/ 117 cm)

AFRICAN DONKEYS
These donkeys are drinking from a water hole in Kenya, where they are living semiwild on a ranch. They must fend for themselves and learn to keep away from leopards, hyenas, and other predators, just as other wild animals have to do.

DONKEYS OF IRELAND
Donkeys are the traditional pack and work animals of Ireland, one of the few countries in northern Europe where they have been bred for hundreds of years and have become adapted to a climate that is very different from the deserts where they evolved. Irish donkeys have much shorter legs than the donkeys from the hotter Mediterranean and Arabian regions, and they have much thicker coats so they can survive the cold.

Long ears

Long tail, with tuft at tip

Well-trimmed hooves

REGAL WHITE DONKEYS
Donkeys are now popular as pets for children and on farms. This has led to breeding for new looks, like these white donkeys with curly coats. In the ancient world white donkeys were the favored mounts of royalty.

Mules and hinnies

T HE SUMERIANS OF MESOPOTAMIA were the first people to interbreed horses and donkeys to produce mules (donkey father, horse mother) and hinnies (horse father, donkey mother) about 4,000 years ago. Roman writers on agriculture told how donkey stallions kept for mule-breeding were brought up with horses so that they would mate more readily with the mares. For thousands of years, mules have been used as pack animals (pp. 46–47) to carry huge loads, because they combine the donkey's stamina with the horse's strength. Like its parents, a mule is a herd animal that travels best in a "mule train" (a long line of mules harnessed together to pull loads). A "bell mare" (a specially trained female horse with a bell around her neck) would lead the mules, who learned to follow the bell's sound, so they could travel at night without being lost in the dark. The horse family is unusual in that all the species can interbreed. Although the resulting offspring will grow to be healthy animals, they are usually sterile.

Breast collar (easier to fit than larger collar, as chest is so narrow)

Long, asslike ears of its father

During a hard day's travel, a working mule feeds from a nose bag filled with oats

ANCIENT EGYPTIAN EQUIDS
This ancient Egyptian tomb painting (c. 1400 B.C.) shows a pair of horses drawing a chariot; below, two white hinnies are also pulling one. Their smaller ears show they are hinnies, not mules, and the straight neck, dark cross on the shoulders, and tufted tail indicate they are not horses.

Crate of ducks

Large wheel makes it easier for donkey to pull this load

INDIAN TRAVEL
Mule carts are still used in Asia and have remained unchanged for at least 3,000 years. However, the method of harnessing has changed, for the earliest carts were always attached to a pair of mules or horses with a central wood pole. The idea of putting a single animal between two wood shafts was not invented until 2,000 years ago. Here the mule has a bridle with a bit, and it is driven with reins. All the family's goods are piled into the cart, including their ducks.

14-year-old mule, 13.3 hands (55 in/140 cm), drawing Indian cart (c. 1840)

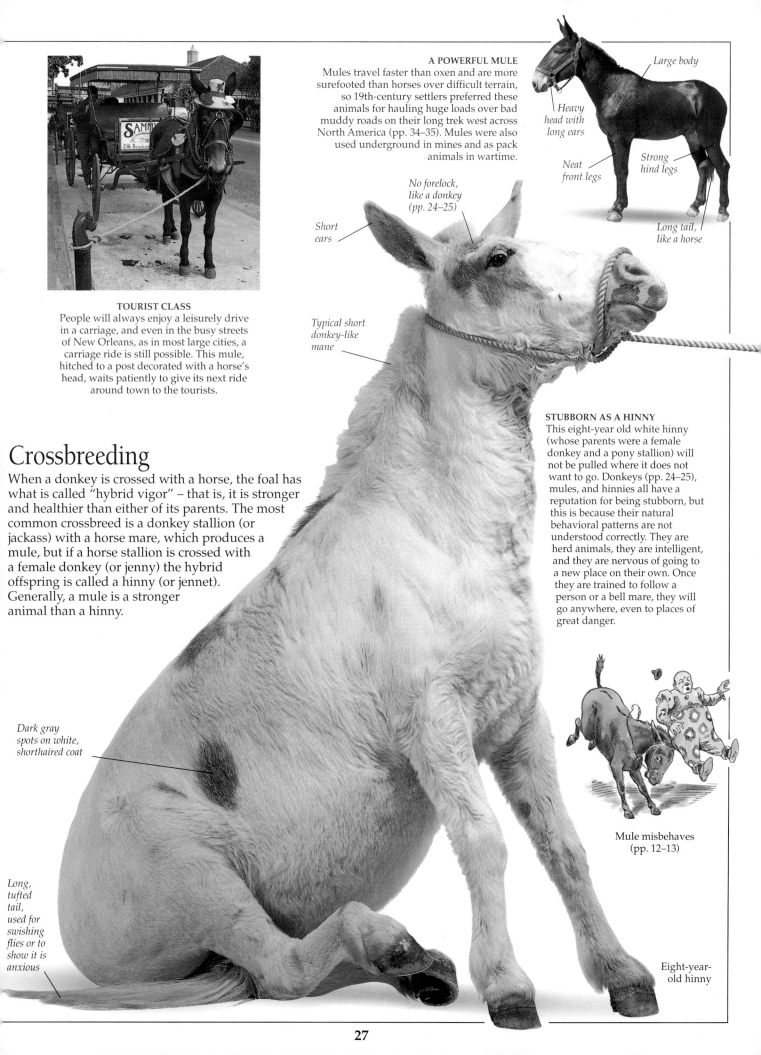

A POWERFUL MULE

Mules travel faster than oxen and are more surefooted than horses over difficult terrain, so 19th-century settlers preferred these animals for hauling huge loads over bad muddy roads on their long trek west across North America (pp. 34–35). Mules were also used underground in mines and as pack animals in wartime.

Large body

Heavy head with long ears

Neat front legs

Strong hind legs

Long tail, like a horse

TOURIST CLASS

People will always enjoy a leisurely drive in a carriage, and even in the busy streets of New Orleans, as in most large cities, a carriage ride is still possible. This mule, hitched to a post decorated with a horse's head, waits patiently to give its next ride around town to the tourists.

No forelock, like a donkey (pp. 24–25)

Short ears

Typical short donkey-like mane

Crossbreeding

When a donkey is crossed with a horse, the foal has what is called "hybrid vigor" – that is, it is stronger and healthier than either of its parents. The most common crossbreed is a donkey stallion (or jackass) with a horse mare, which produces a mule, but if a horse stallion is crossed with a female donkey (or jenny) the hybrid offspring is called a hinny (or jennet). Generally, a mule is a stronger animal than a hinny.

STUBBORN AS A HINNY

This eight-year old white hinny (whose parents were a female donkey and a pony stallion) will not be pulled where it does not want to go. Donkeys (pp. 24–25), mules, and hinnies all have a reputation for being stubborn, but this is because their natural behavioral patterns are not understood correctly. They are herd animals, they are intelligent, and they are nervous of going to a new place on their own. Once they are trained to follow a person or a bell mare, they will go anywhere, even to places of great danger.

Dark gray spots on white, shorthaired coat

Mule misbehaves
(pp. 12–13)

Long, tufted tail, used for swishing flies or to show it is anxious

Eight-year-old hinny

27

Shoes and shoeing

Old horseshoe and nails just removed from horse's hoof by blacksmith

THE HOOVES OF ALL EQUIDS are made from keratin, a protein that is the same organic (natural) substance as hair or human fingernails. Just like hair and nails, the hooves can be cut and shaped without discomfort to the animal. The hooves of a domestic horse wear down evenly if it is ridden over flat, hard ground, but if the land is rocky, the hooves may split and chip. If the ground is muddy and soft, the hooves may grow too long and become diseased. It is necessary, therefore, for the horse to have regular attention from a blacksmith, a person specially trained to look after hooves and fit them with metal shoes for protection. The hoof is made up of three parts – the wall, or outer part, to which the shoe is attached with nails; the sole; and the frog, the wedge-shaped part at the center.

1 REMOVE OLD SHOE
The horse stands patiently while the farrier carefully levers off the worn old shoe.

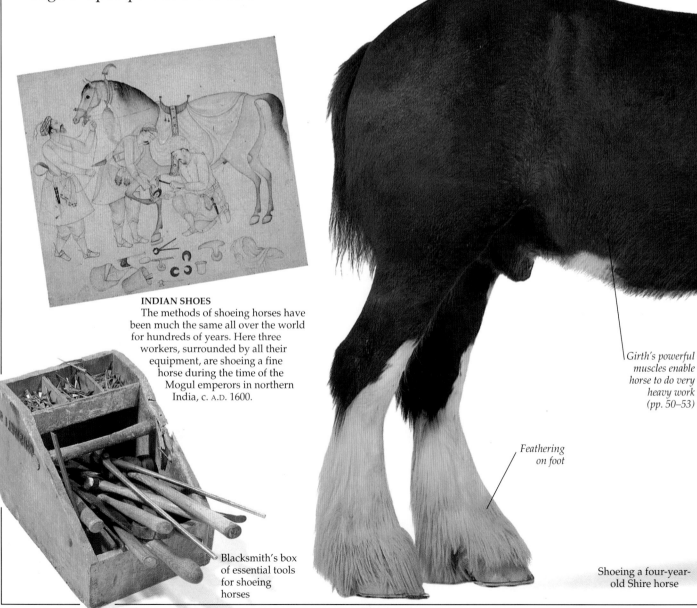

INDIAN SHOES
The methods of shoeing horses have been much the same all over the world for hundreds of years. Here three workers, surrounded by all their equipment, are shoeing a fine horse during the time of the Mogul emperors in northern India, c. A.D. 1600.

Girth's powerful muscles enable horse to do very heavy work (pp. 50–53)

Feathering on foot

Blacksmith's box of essential tools for shoeing horses

Shoeing a four-year-old Shire horse

GAME OF LUCK
All over the world, the horseshoe is a talisman for good luck. It must always be held with the open part at the top so that the good luck will not drop out. Horseshoe pitching – a game based on luck – is a popular pastime in the U.S. and Canada. Shown here is an iron horseshoe (c. 1st century A.D.), found in southern England.

Horseshoe-shaped growth, removed by blacksmith along with old shoe

2 CLEANING THE HOOF
The worn layer of the sole is clipped off, the new layer is filed down, and the whole hoof is cleaned and made ready for the new shoe.

3 SHAPING UP
The new iron shoe for the hoof is made red hot in the furnace at 2,000°F (1,090°C). Using a heavy hammer, the blacksmith shapes the shoe on his anvil.

4 STEAMING
After the shoe has been reheated, it is pressed onto the hoof to check the fit and then allowed to cool. The hoof gives off a smell of burning hair and much smoke, but this does not hurt the horse.

Height at withers 17.2 hands (70 in/ 178 cm)

Chestnut

6 FINISHED FOOT
The rim of the foot is then filed, as is the hoof just under the nail ends, before the blacksmith hammers them flat. The nails should be flush with the shoe, and the hoof and the outside edge of the shoe should match precisely.

Balancing on one front foot

Filing hoof and nail ends flat

5 NAILING ON THE SHOE
Then the blacksmith takes some special iron nails and hammers them through the predrilled holes in the shoe. The nail ends that show through the horse's hoof are cut off and bent back.

WHEN "HIPPO" MEANT "HORSE"
Iron horseshoes were invented after the Roman period, but the Romans often tied a shoe made of wicker or metal onto the hoof with leather straps. This was called a "hipposandal," from the Greek *hippo* meaning "horse."

Hipposandal, French, 1st–3rd century A.D.

Bits and pieces

THE EARLIEST DOMESTIC horses and asses were probably ridden bareback and guided by a rope that was tied around the lower jaw in the gap between the cheek teeth and the incisors. Today this remains a common way of controlling donkeys in Turkey and Greece. The first bits, or mouthpieces of the bridle, were made of hide, bone, or wood and had fastenings at each end to which reins were attached. Beginning c. 1500 B.C. bits were made of bronze, and later iron. Until late Roman times, riders did not use saddles – they rode bareback or on a horse cloth – and there were no stirrups (loops suspended from a horse's saddle to support rider's foot) in Europe until the 8th century A.D. The lack of saddles and stirrups did not prevent either Eurasian riders, or later, Native Americans (pp. 56–57) from holding their bows and shooting arrows from a galloping horse. The most powerful nomadic horse riders in the ancient world were the Scythians (pp. 32–33) from central Asia in the 5th and 4th centuries B.C. They had very elaborate harnesses, but they still rode with only a single saddle cloth and no stirrups. These horses were the riders' most valuable possessions and were buried with them in their tombs.

Back view of woman riding sidesaddle

JINGLE BELLS
Bells on the harness were a safety feature. If horses and passengers became lost in snow-covered countryside, the bells' chimes would let rescuers know their position.

SPURRED ON
The horses of the Middle Ages in 13th-century Europe had a very hard time, for they were bridled with bits and goaded by armored knights wearing cruel spurs (U-shaped devices attached to heel of rider's boot, pp. 44–45). These were either prickspurs or rowel spurs with little wheels.

Rowel spur (9.1 in/23 cm), made of iron and brass, western Europe, early 1500s

Rowel

Screw would have clamped stirrup to outside of shoe

Metal part of stirrup would have fitted inside heel of shoe

Tiny rowel spur (1.6 in/4 cm), made of iron and fitting directly onto shoe, Europe, late 1600s

Buckle for attaching stirrup to boot

Metal part of stirrup for "pricking" horse

Prickspur (11.4 in/29 cm), made of iron, N.W. Africa (Moorish), early 1800s

PUTTING YOUR FOOT IN IT
It is thought that the Chinese invented metal foot stirrups in the 5th century A.D. Stirrups then spread slowly westward to Europe. The use of stirrups altered the way battles were fought (pp. 44–45), because they allowed riders to wield their weapons without falling off.

Iron stirrup, Bulgaria, A.D. 800–900

Decorated boot stirrup, made of iron, Spain, 1600s

Brass fretwork

Box stirrup, made of painted wood and brass fretwork, France or Italy, late 1700s

Dragon decoration

Brass stirrup, decorated with two dragons, China, 1800s

Jointed snaffle bit,
Ireland, 100 B.C.–A.D. 100

Joint

Rein ring

BUILD A BETTER BIT

Three types of bit have been invented for controlling domesticated horses. The first is the simple "snaffle" bit, which developed into a jointed mouthpiece in Assyria, c. 900 B.C. A "curb" bit is unjointed with a chain running under the horse's chin, which applies pressure when the reins are used. The third bit is a "pelham," which combines the two bits of a double bridle into one. It has a curb chain and can be used with one or two reins.

DEFEAT IN BATTLE

In the Battle of Hastings, 1066, the 7,000 troops brought over from Normandy by William the Conqueror fought against the English. One reason why they won the war was that they fought on horseback with the new invention of stirrups, while the English dismounted and fought in the old way on foot.

Detail from the Bayeux tapestry from France, c. 1080

Jointed snaffle bit with cheekpiece, Bulgaria, A.D. 800–900

Joint

Rein ring

Cheekpiece

Curb bit (length 12 in/305 mm, width 2 in/50 mm), made of steel and brass, Europe, 1500s

Curb chain

Double rollers in horse's mouth

Rein ring

Brass boss

Curb bit (length 7.3 in/185 mm, width 4.3 in/110 mm), made of steel and brass, Portugal, 1800s

Brass boss

Rein ring

Curb chain

Mouthpiece

Brow-band

Crownpiece

Throatlatch

Rein

Bit

Height at withers 17 hands (68 in/173 cm)

RIDING SIDESADDLE

This gray Lipizzaner gelding is being ridden sidesaddle. Women today usually only ride like this in the show ring or when hunting. In former times, from the early 1300s onward, the sidesaddle was the only way a female rider, wearing long, heavy skirts, could be mounted on a horse.

Girth

Safety stirrup

Rider on leather saddle made-to-measure in 1890

Woman, in Victorian dress, riding sidesaddle on a six-year-old Lipizzaner

Rein ring (terret), England, 1st century A.D.

Strap-union made of bronze (for joining straps together), England, 1st century A.D.

Decorated terret (a ring on saddle harness through which driving reins pass), found in Egypt, 1st century B.C.

Exploring by horse

WITHOUT THE HORSE AND THE ASS, human history would have been quite different. Civilizations would have evolved in their places of origin and their peoples would not have traveled around the world in search of new places to explore and conquer. There would have been no Crusades, and Europeans could not have destroyed the indigenous cultures of the Americas. An invading force has to have fast transportation and efficient movement of goods, weapons, and food, otherwise it is powerless against the defenses of settled communities. Although horseback riding was the general means of transportation from at least 1000 B.C., it was not until 2000 years later, in the 11th century A.D., that horses were commonly shod and a saddle and stirrups widely used. From this time onward, the horse became increasingly important in war and sports (pp. 42–45), and travelers like Marco Polo could ride huge distances across Europe and Asia – journeys that today would be considered long even by airplane.

VIKING CHESSMAN
This knight on horseback, carved from a walrus tusk during the 12th century, is one of the famous chessmen found on the Isle of Lewis off Scotland's west coast.

GENGHIS KHAN
Genghis Khan (A.D. 1162–1227), the Mongolian conqueror, ruled an empire of nomadic horsemen that stretched across Asia into Europe – from the Pacific Ocean to the Black Sea.

Pair of bronze Etruscan riders, c. 500 B.C.

Statue of Charlemagne, the Holy Roman Emperor

ARCHERS OF THE ANCIENT WORLD
These two elegant Etruscan bronzes from northern Italy, c. 500 B.C., show how – even without saddle and stirrups – Scythian archers could shoot their arrows from a galloping horse. The archer shooting backward exemplifies the "Parthian shot," a technique commonly used by the nomadic horsemen on the steppes of central Asia.

HOLY ROMAN EMPEROR
Charlemagne, or Charles the Great (A.D. 742–814), was the most famous ruler of the Middle Ages. As emperor of the Frankish kingdom, he conquered Saxony and Lombardy. In A.D. 796 he led over 15,000 horsemen against the Avars in Hungary. In A.D. 800 he was crowned Emperor of the Holy Roman Empire, stretching from Denmark to central Italy, from France to Austria.

Fretwork

IN THE SADDLE
This 18th-century Tibetan wood saddle, decorated with gold and silver fretwork, may have been similar to one owned by Genghis Khan 600 years earlier.

Tree

Cantle

Pommel

18th-century Tibetan saddle

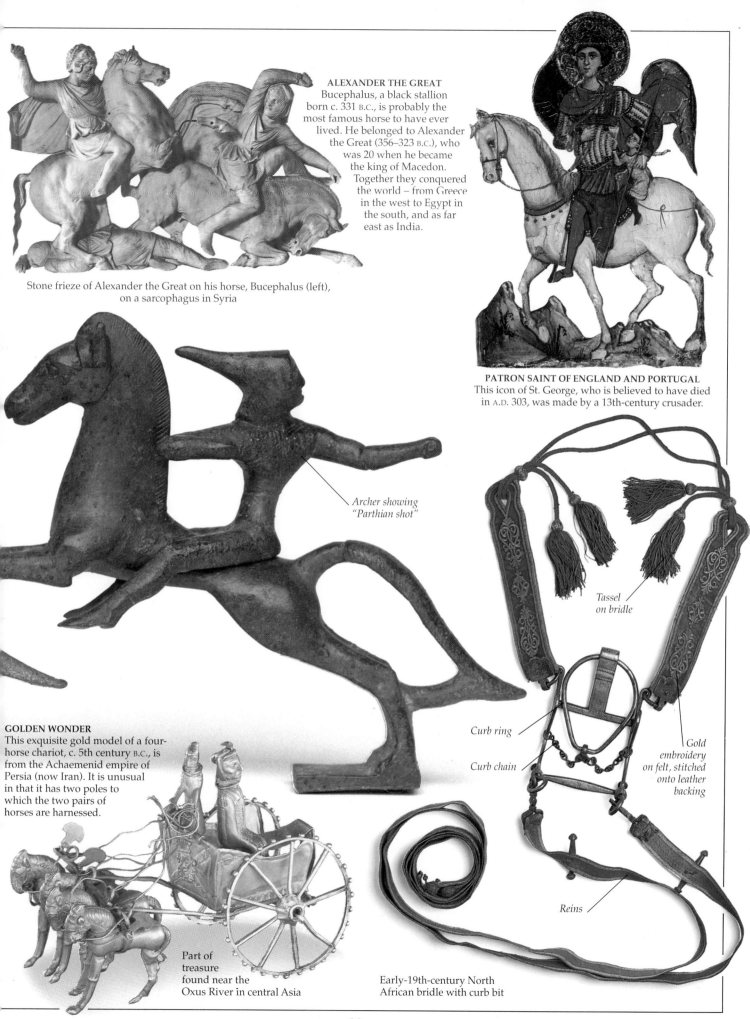

ALEXANDER THE GREAT
Bucephalus, a black stallion born c. 331 B.C., is probably the most famous horse to have ever lived. He belonged to Alexander the Great (356–323 B.C.), who was 20 when he became the king of Macedon. Together they conquered the world – from Greece in the west to Egypt in the south, and as far east as India.

Stone frieze of Alexander the Great on his horse, Bucephalus (left), on a sarcophagus in Syria

PATRON SAINT OF ENGLAND AND PORTUGAL
This icon of St. George, who is believed to have died in A.D. 303, was made by a 13th-century crusader.

Archer showing "Parthian shot"

Tassel on bridle

Curb ring

Curb chain

Gold embroidery on felt, stitched onto leather backing

Reins

GOLDEN WONDER
This exquisite gold model of a four-horse chariot, c. 5th century B.C., is from the Achaemenid empire of Persia (now Iran). It is unusual in that it has two poles to which the two pairs of horses are harnessed.

Part of treasure found near the Oxus River in central Asia

Early-19th-century North African bridle with curb bit

To the Americas

FINE HATS
For ceremonial occasions the Sioux chieftains, from America's northern plains, wear their finest headdresses, made of wild turkey feathers, and ride their most beautiful horses.

Bᴇꜰᴏʀᴇ 1492, when the first European settlers arrived in both North and South America, the continents were densely populated with native peoples, who had arrived there between 20,000 and 10,000 years earlier. The European invaders had a fast means of transportation for people and supplies – the horse and the mule.

THE BLACK HAWK WAR
Like other North American nations, the Sa[u]k of the northern Mississippi River prized th[e] horses, using them for transport, hunting, in war. Keokuk (above, c. 1760–1848), who been appointed Sauk chief U.S. officials, signed treaties giving away much of the Sa[uk] land. Black Hawk, the Sauks leader, and his people fiercel[y] defended their land, but w[ere] defeated in the end. By millions of acres of I[ndian] territory were ced[ed] European settle[rs]

Therefore, they were able to conquer the Native Americans and take over vast areas of land. Soon a few horses escaped to live and breed in the wild. Within a hundred years they had spread over all the grasslands (pp. 36–37). The Native Americans of both continents quickly realized the value of the horse. By bartering with the Spanish, they obtained their own stock, which they learned to ride with as much dexterity as the ancient Scythians, who could shoot an arrow from a bow while riding a galloping horse without stirrups (pp. 32–33).

Blaze

Central wood shaft, or "tongue," to which harness is attached

BEASTS OF BURDEN
Before there were railroads across the North American continent, teams of six or more mules (pp. 26–27) would haul heavily laden wagons along roads that were often deep in mud and impassable by any other means of transportation.

Martingale

Stocking

DOWN MEXICO WAY
In the early 1500s, Spanish conquistadores brought horses (similar to Andalusians, pp. 40–41) to the New World, where they had been extinct for 10,000 years. Here Indians present Hernando Cortés (1485–1547), the conqueror of Mexico, with a treasured necklace.

Shod hoof, giving better grip in soft earth

WESTWARD, HO!
Trappers, traders, and missionaries were the first to reach the Pacific, but in 1843 a determined band of 1,000 settlers left Missouri on the 2,000-mile (3,300-km) trek westward along the Oregon Trail. To protect themselves from attack, they would form their wagons into a circle at dusk. Finally after many grueling months, bad weather, disease, poor food, and crossing the Rocky Mountains, they reached their destination.

Canvas held up by iron hoop underneath

Waterproofed heavy-duty canvas top

Brake lever

Axle supporting massive weight of wagon and its load

Iron rim over wood wheel

Whiffletree, attaching harness to wagon

Metal hub

Trace

Pair of Gelderlands 16.2 hands (66 in/168 cm) pulling prairie schooner

AMERICA'S FIRST MOBILE HOME
The early European settlers traveled across North America with their children and all their belongings in a covered wagon, or prairie schooner. It was a hard life for they had to be entirely self-sufficient, knowing how to shoe a horse (pp. 28–29), mend a wheel, bake bread, and nurse the sick.

Front wheel, 4 ft (123 cm) across, is smaller to allow sharp turning

SOUTHERN COWBOY
The horsemen, or gauchos, of the South American pampas work mainly on huge ranches. Like the cowboys of North America, they spend their lives in the saddle, expertly rounding up cattle.

Running wild

THERE ARE NO LONGER ANY TRULY WILD HORSES living in the wild, but all over the world there are many herds of horses and ponies that are considered "feral." Feral animals are descended from domesticated (tamed) stock but are no longer under human control, and they live and breed in the wild. The last truly wild horses were the Przewalski horses (pp. 20–21), which survived in small numbers on the Mongolian steppes (plains) until the 1960s. At the end of the 15th century, horses spread rapidly over the grasslands of North and South America soon after the first Europeans arrived (pp. 34–35), bringing their mounts with them. Soon there were millions of horses living wild. Today, the number of feral horses – for example, the mustang of North America and the Australian brumby – is much less than in the past. The population is controlled – some are killed by hunters, and others are rounded up and domesticated.

FELL PONIES
In Britain there are many breeds of pony that live on the moors, like the Fell pony. Although Fell ponies are domesticated, they are allowed to live and breed with very little human control. Traditionally, Fell ponies have been used as pack ponies, for riding, and for light draft work.

GERMAN DÜLMEN
These rare ponies live semiwild on the Duke of Croy's estate in Westphalia, Germany. They have been crossbred with both British and Polish ponies, so they are not purebred. The herd dates back to the early 1300s.

Long ears

Well-proportioned head

Coat colors vary from bay, brown, and gray, but never piebald or skewbald (pp. 38–41)

Strong legs support sturdy, well-built body

Strong horny hooves

THE BRUMBY OF AUSTRALIA
For 150 years there have been herds of feral horses in Australia, ever since they were abandoned during the gold rush. These horses, called brumbies, formed herds and reproduced in great numbers over large areas. They are unpopular with cattle and sheep ranchers because they compete for grazing and usually carry many parasites. Since the 1960s, they have been hunted so extensively that there are now very few.

SYMBOLIC HORSES
A wild running horse has often been used as a symbol of freedom and elegance. It has advertised many things, from banks to sports cars – such as the Mustang and Pinto in the U.S. and (as shown here) the Ferrari, the supreme speedster.

Ferrari

THE MUSTANGS OF AMERICA
The feral horses, or mustangs, of the Nevada desert have hard lives traveling great distances in search of enough grass and water to live on.

DAWN IN THE CAMARGUE
The beautiful white horses from the Camargue in the south of France have lived wild in the marshes of the Rhone delta for over a thousand years. They have very wide hooves for living on soft wet grassland.

Short stripe on face

Star

Long, straight, full mane

Snip

Deep girth

Full forelock

THE PONIES OF THE NEW FOREST
In Britain there have been herds of ponies living in the New Forest woodlands of Hampshire, England, since the 11th century. For 700 years these ponies lived wild there, but in the 18th and 19th centuries attempts were made to increase their size by bringing in stallions of other breeds. They still run wild in their native area, but also are reared on private stud farms to provide ideal ponies for children and adults to ride and for light draft work (pp. 54–55).

New Forest ponies range in height from 12.2 to 14.2 hands (127–147 cm)

Blaze

Horses from around the world

Gray coat is black skin, with a mixture of white and black hairs, as in this Connemara pony from Ireland

Dapple gray occurs when dark gray hairs form rings on a gray coat, as in this Orlov Trotter from Russia

Palomino (a color, not a breed) is a gold coat, with white mane and tail, as in this Haflinger pony from Austria

THE DIFFERENT BREEDS OF HORSE are often divided by breeders into three types. First are "hotbloods," or "fullbloods" – the Arabian and Thoroughbred breeds. These horses have the same blood temperature as other breeds, so they do not really have "hot blood"; they are given the name because of their high-spirited temperament and because they are descended from the Arabian and Barb breeds from the hot countries of North Africa and Arabia. Second are "coldbloods," which again do not have cold blood but are the large, heavy, calm, draft horses (pp. 50–53) from cold, northern climates. Third are "warmbloods," or "crossbreeds," which are crosses between hotbloods and coldbloods. It is this group that supplies most modern sporting horses (pp. 59–61), except for racehorses, which are almost always Thoroughbreds. All Thorough-breds' ancestry can be traced back to three famous stallions – the Byerly Turk (c. 1689), the Darley Arabian (c. 1705), and the Godolphin Arabian (c. 1728).

Chestnut is various shades of reddish brown, as in this French Trotter from Normandy, France

Decorated bridle

Height at withers 14.3 hands (59 in/ 150 cm)

Four-year-old, purebred Arabian, mahogany bay in color

Bay is a reddish coat, with black mane, tail, and "points" (ears, legs, and muzzle), as in this Cleveland Bay from England

A coronet is the white hair just above the hoof

A sock is the white hair reaching halfway up the cannon bone

Brown is mixed black and brown in coat with brown mane, tail and legs, as in this Nonius from Hungary

A stocking is the white hair reaching up to the knee or the hock (pp. 10–11)

BARBS AND BERBERS
The Barb, second only to the Arabian as the world's first horse breed, has long been the traditional mount of North African tribesmen (Berbers). Here Moroccan horsemen display their riding skills at a festival.

Height at withers 14.1 hands (57 in/145 cm)

COATS OF MANY COLORS
In this elaborate painting of a Persian fable, made by Indian artists during the Mogul rule (c. 1590), a crow is addressing an assembly of animals. They include several horses in a variety of coat colors – chestnut, light and dappled grays, bay, and skewbald (pp. 40–41).

REARING UP
Because horses are so beautiful and can be trained so easily, they are indispensable for circus entertainment. They seem to enjoy carrying out difficult and unusual movements with their bodies, as shown here.

15-year-old Arabian, very light gray color with tiny dapples in coat

HORSE FAIR
For many centuries, horses have been bought and sold at horse sales around the world, as shown in this detail of a painting by English artist John Herring (1795–1865).

ARISTOCRATIC ARABIAN
The Arabian is the aristocrat of horses with its elegant head, slender limbs, high carriage of the tail, and fiery temperament. Arabians have been carefully bred and records kept of their pedigrees for over a thousand years in their countries of origin in North Africa and Arabia.

Embroidered saddlecloth

39

More breeds and colors

EVERY COUNTRY HAS ITS OWN BREED OF HORSE – from India's polo pony, to southern Africa's Basuto pony, and England's Shire horse (pp. 50–53). Each breed is adapted to life in its place of origin and each has its own uses. The breeds are defined by their "conformation," or size and body shape, as well as by their color and any white markings they may have on their faces and legs. Horses come in many different sizes – from the smallest horse in the world, the Falabella, which measures no more than 7.2 hh (30 in/76 cm) at the withers, to the largest of all breeds, the Shire horse. A Shire stallion should be 16.2 hh (66 in/168 cm) or above, and should weigh about a ton. Shires are usually black or bay with a white blaze on their forehead, or gray. Their heavily feathered feet have white socks or stockings (pp. 38–39). There are many sayings linking horses' behavior with their coat colors. There is an Arab saying that all horses but bays are unlucky, unless they have white markings, and another that a white horse is the most princely but that it suffers from the heat. There is a widespread belief, too, that chestnuts are fast but hot tempered.

Height at withers 16.1 hands (65 in/ 165 cm)

Flat metal stirrup

STARS...
It is usual for horses to have white markings on their faces, such as a regular or irregular star shape set high on the face between the eyes. An example is this Danish Warmblood, a breed now regarded as Denmark's national horse. A small white patch between the nostrils is called a snip.

...AND STRIPES
A long, narrow strip of white, extending from above the eyes to the nostrils, is called a stripe, as on this Oldenburg, a breed first established in Germany in the 1600s. A stripe can also be interrupted, with the coat color showing between the star, short stripe, and snip down the horse's face.

WHAT THE BLAZES!
A wide strip starting above the eyes and extending down to the muzzle is called a blaze, as on this Gelderland from the Netherlands, a breed that has existed for the last century. When white hair covers almost all the face from the forelock to the lips, it is called a bald face.

Seven-year-old dark gray purebred Andalusian ridden by a woman in classical Spanish riding costume

CLASSICAL EQUITATION
The Spanish Riding School was founded in 1572, when nine Lipizzaner stallions and 24 mares were brought to Vienna in Austria from Spain.

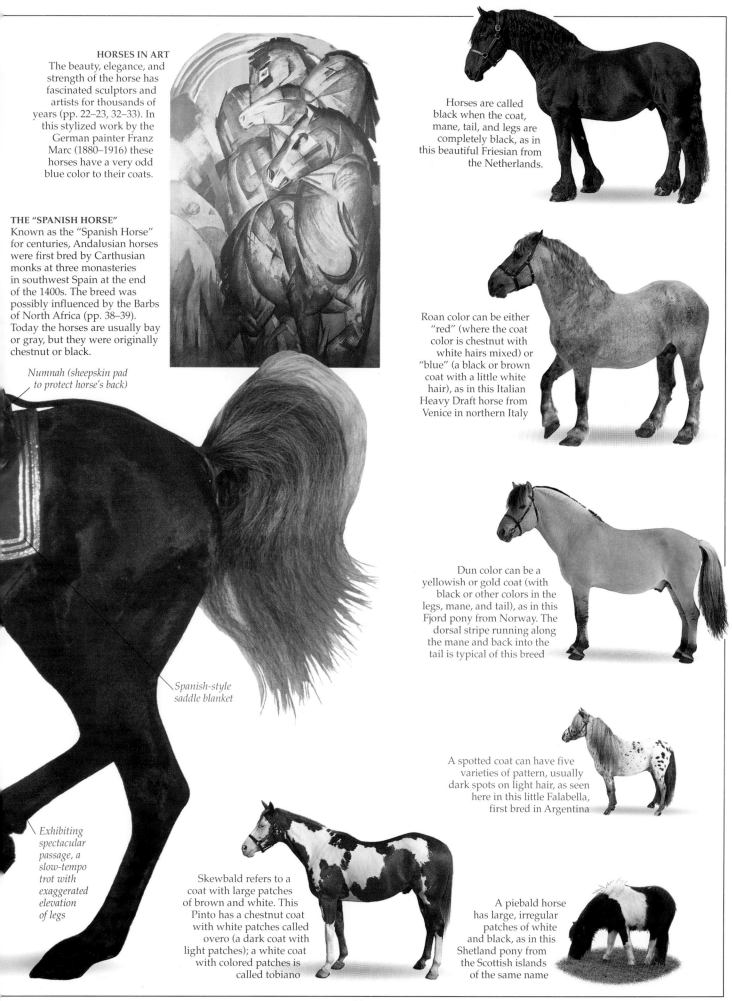

HORSES IN ART
The beauty, elegance, and strength of the horse has fascinated sculptors and artists for thousands of years (pp. 22–23, 32–33). In this stylized work by the German painter Franz Marc (1880–1916) these horses have a very odd blue color to their coats.

THE "SPANISH HORSE"
Known as the "Spanish Horse" for centuries, Andalusian horses were first bred by Carthusian monks at three monasteries in southwest Spain at the end of the 1400s. The breed was possibly influenced by the Barbs of North Africa (pp. 38–39). Today the horses are usually bay or gray, but they were originally chestnut or black.

Numnah (sheepskin pad to protect horse's back)

Spanish-style saddle blanket

Exhibiting spectacular passage, a slow-tempo trot with exaggerated elevation of legs

Horses are called black when the coat, mane, tail, and legs are completely black, as in this beautiful Friesian from the Netherlands.

Roan color can be either "red" (where the coat color is chestnut with white hairs mixed) or "blue" (a black or brown coat with a little white hair), as in this Italian Heavy Draft horse from Venice in northern Italy

Dun color can be a yellowish or gold coat (with black or other colors in the legs, mane, and tail), as in this Fjord pony from Norway. The dorsal stripe running along the mane and back into the tail is typical of this breed

A spotted coat can have five varieties of pattern, usually dark spots on light hair, as seen here in this little Falabella, first bred in Argentina

Skewbald refers to a coat with large patches of brown and white. This Pinto has a chestnut coat with white patches called overo (a dark coat with light patches); a white coat with colored patches is called tobiano

A piebald horse has large, irregular patches of white and black, as in this Shetland pony from the Scottish islands of the same name

War-horses

THE HORSE AND THE ASS have been used to assist humans in their wars of invasion for the last 5,000 years. By riding in chariots harnessed to a pair of horses, people could travel much faster than on foot and could cause much greater damage to the enemy. At first the "wars" were small squabbles between individuals, but then families grew larger and settled into villages, and battles sometimes took place between the villages. From the time of Alexander the Great (pp. 32–33), when armed horse riders (cavalry) developed, the horse played a major role in all wars until just after World War I, when mechanized vehicles took over. After stirrups became widespread in Europe in the early medieval period, the cavalry was better able to protect themselves and fight more efficiently because the stirrups and new, higher saddles gave a steadier seat; and riders were able to use longer weapons like lances. This meant that armor had to be heavier and horses had to be bred larger and stronger, but they were never as large as the heavy horses of today.

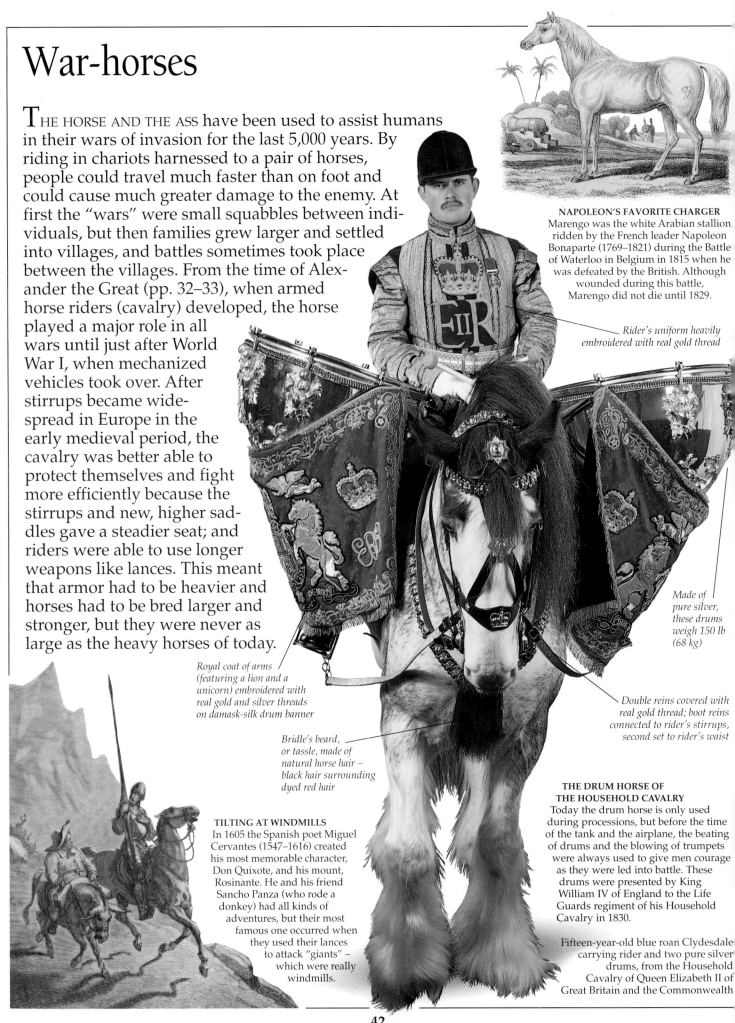

NAPOLEON'S FAVORITE CHARGER
Marengo was the white Arabian stallion ridden by the French leader Napoleon Bonaparte (1769–1821) during the Battle of Waterloo in Belgium in 1815 when he was defeated by the British. Although wounded during this battle, Marengo did not die until 1829.

Rider's uniform heavily embroidered with real gold thread

Made of pure silver, these drums weigh 150 lb (68 kg)

Royal coat of arms (featuring a lion and a unicorn) embroidered with real gold and silver threads on damask-silk drum banner

Bridle's beard, or tassle, made of natural horse hair – black hair surrounding dyed red hair

Double reins covered with real gold thread; boot reins connected to rider's stirrups, second set to rider's waist

TILTING AT WINDMILLS
In 1605 the Spanish poet Miguel Cervantes (1547–1616) created his most memorable character, Don Quixote, and his mount, Rosinante. He and his friend Sancho Panza (who rode a donkey) had all kinds of adventures, but their most famous one occurred when they used their lances to attack "giants" – which were really windmills.

THE DRUM HORSE OF THE HOUSEHOLD CAVALRY
Today the drum horse is only used during processions, but before the time of the tank and the airplane, the beating of drums and the blowing of trumpets were always used to give men courage as they were led into battle. These drums were presented by King William IV of England to the Life Guards regiment of his Household Cavalry in 1830.

Fifteen-year-old blue roan Clydesdale carrying rider and two pure silver drums, from the Household Cavalry of Queen Elizabeth II of Great Britain and the Commonwealth

INTO BATTLE
The Charge of the Light Brigade – which resulted in huge casualties of both horses and men – was the most disastrous battle of the Crimean War (1853–1856), fought between Russia on one side and Britain, Turkey, France, and Sardinia on the other. The Crimea is a small area of land to the north of the Black Sea in the Ukraine.

Red Cross flag

The first ambulances, like this one from World War I, were harnessed to a pair of horses or mules

Whiffletree to which horse's harness was hitched to vehicle

Brake

Small front wheel to allow sharp turning

Large rear wheel to carry heavy loads

TIBETAN WARRIOR
For hundreds of years, the Tibetan cavalry used a form of armor made of small metal plates (lamellae) laced together with leather thongs. This type of armor, for both horse and rider, had been used by the nomadic warriors of central Asia and was very similar to that worn by the Mongols when they overran Asia and Eastern Europe (pp. 32–33). The Tibetans have preserved this traditional armor – even into the 20th century.

Metal chanfron for protecting horse's head

Crinet for protecting horse's neck

Peytral to protect horse's chest

Leather lace

Small metal plate

Crupper protecting horse's hind quarters

Tibetan cavalry armor, for horse and rider, used between the 17th and 19th centuries

AUSTRALIAN ARTILLERY
The Waler (named after New South Wales in Australia, where horses were first imported 200 years ago) was the world's finest cavalry horse during World War I. These horses were strong and hardy and had good stamina and an amiable temperament. Now the Australian Stock Horse, based on the Waler, is used widely on cattle stations (ranches) for herding.

Nineteenth-century British cavalry spur, made of nickel silver

NECESSITIES OF WAR
No battle could be fought without supplies of food, water, and arms hauled to the front line by pack-horses and mules.

Metal barrel containing water for either troops or animals

Whiffletree

Tongue

World War I water wagon hauled by two horses, made in England and used in France

STURDY STIRRUPS
The stirrup was the most important innovation in the history of the horse in war, because it enabled a heavily armed rider to stay on his horse. Shown here is an 18th-century British cavalry stirrup made of brass.

GHANIAN WARRIOR
This brass model of a warrior on horseback was cast in Ghana in West Africa during the 18th century.

The age of chivalry

The politics of europe was dominated by the feudal system during the 11th and 12th centuries. Some knights were feudal lords, who owned tracts of land and granted its use to their vassals. They also owned serfs, over whom they had complete power. These knights were Christians, bound by the code of chivalry – a religious, moral, and social code that covered every aspect of their lives. The ideal knight was brave, courteous, and honorable, and totally dedicated to war against all non-Christians. By 1200, much of Europe was settled under feudalism, and armed knights began the conquest of new lands in the east. The Crusades were fought over territory, but religious passion and the principles of chivalry meant that leaders, such as Richard the Lion-Heart, could depend on their armed knights to give up their lives for the cause of winning Jerusalem from the Muslims.

SAMURAI WARRIOR
This screen painting depicts a 12th-century Japanese samurai warrior going into battle. The honorable samurai, who wore two swords and a distinctive headdress, was totally loyal to his feudal lord.

European late 19th-century brass copy of 15th-century medieval spur with rowel (pp. 30–31), which had to be long to reach under the horse's armor

Lambrequin, or mantling

Leather gauntlet, or glove

Blunted wood lance

Cloth surcoat

Caparison, a colorfully decorated horse covering

Chain-mail armor

THE ROMANCE OF THE JOUST
Armed knights learned how to fight on horseback in tournaments. This sport, known as "justing," or "jousting" (from the Latin *juxtare*, meaning to clash), was part of the code of chivalry. The heavily armed knights tried to win points by either unhorsing their opponents or by breaking their own lances (up to 8 ft/2.5 m long) against the other's shields. From the dangerous hand-to-hand fighting, or melees, of the 12th century to the colorful pageantry of the 15th and 16th centuries, competitive tournaments were very popular spectator sports until their decline during the 17th century.

Reconstruction of a pair of sporting jousters from the early 14th century

ARMOR FIT FOR A KING
Henry VIII of England passed laws to increase the size of horses by preventing the breeding of small stock. At the time of his reign in the early 1500s, the cannon had taken over as the principal weapon of war, against which heavy armor was no defense, but this armor was still used in royal parades.

This full horse armor (or bard), known as the "Burgundian Bard," was given by Emperor Maximilian I of the Holy Roman Empire to Henry VIII. It was embossed, engraved, and silvered by Henry's Flemish harness gilder, c. 1515.

Bronze eye guard for protecting a horse's face, England, 1st century A.D.

FULL METAL CHANFRON
This 16th-century Turkish chanfron (head armor for a horse) was made of gilt-copper, or tombac. It was part of a monument to the Ottoman Empire (late 1200s to early 1900s) that was set up in Agia Irene, a Byzantine church in Istanbul, Turkey.

Wood or leather crest in the shape of a bird or other animal was sometimes worn here

Metal helm

Vamplate, or metal disk, for protecting hand

LEG GUARD
Wooden German jousting saddle (c. 1500) used with blunted lances in a "joust of peace" (war games). The two bows curved around the knight's thighs and protected him since he wore no leg armor, but he could not be unseated from his mount. Opponents' horses wore "blind" chanfrons; otherwise they would scare.

Pelham bit

Shield painted in heraldic colors, repeated on horse's caparison

COEUR DE LION
Richard the Lion-Hearted (1157–1199) became king of England in 1189. In 1190, he embarked on the Third Crusade to Palestine, where his bravery gave him immortal fame. He returned to England and spent the rest of his life warring against France.

STOP THAT HORSE
Four-spiked, iron caltrops (English, 1st–2nd century A.D.) were placed in the ground to lame the enemy's horses when they stepped on them.

Traveling by horse

Horses, asses, and mules have been used to transport people and their goods from place to place for more than 4,000 years. The first harness and carts had to be made entirely of wood, bone, and leather, until about 3,500 years ago, when people developed the use of copper and bronze, followed by iron about 2,000 years ago. The use of metals for parts of the harness, like rein rings (terrets) and bits, and on carts for the rims of wheels and for hubs and axles, greatly increased the efficiency and speed of transportation, especially in southern Europe and Asia, where the climate is dry. But in northern Europe, with its high rainfall, the packhorse remained the most practical means of travel (especially in winter) until roads were built, first by the Romans, and then not again until late in the Middle Ages (A.D. 1100–1500).

(carriage image, top left)

FIT FOR A QUEEN
This is a replica of Queen Elizabeth I's carriage – the first carriage to be built for the British monarchy. Before this time, royalty had to ride in carts. Made of wood, with steps that folded up to form part of the side, the carriage's padded roof provided protection from the rain.

HIGHWAYMAN AND HORSE
Dick Turpin (1706–1739) was an English highwayman who, according to legend, rode to the city of York in record time on his mount Black Bess.

BAREBACK RIDER
An 11th-century legend records that Lady Godiva rode naked through Coventry in a protest against heavy taxes imposed by her husband.

HORSE FEATHERS
The horses of the native Americans had endless endurance and great stamina for use in both war and hunting. Color and decoration were part of the native Americans' culture. Chiefs of some nations wore magnificent feathered headdresses, and they often adorned their horses as well.

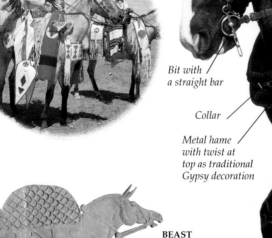

Blinker

Blaze

Bit with a straight bar

Collar

Metal hame with twist at top as traditional Gypsy decoration

Breeching strap

THE TRAVELERS
For hundreds of years, Romany gypsies have traveled around Europe living in their caravans. No one knows where they came from, although they may be of Hindu origin. Today, people like to use these horse-drawn vehicles for holidays.

BEAST OF BURDEN
This stone frieze shows that about 2,600 years ago, the ancient Assyrians bred powerful mules (pp. 26–27) to carry their hunting gear.

46

PATRON SAINT
St. Christopher (3rd century A.D.) was
the patron saint of travelers – his feast
day is July 25. A St. Christopher's
medal has always been a
symbol of good luck.

**PILGRIMS'
PROGRESS**
Pilgrims to
Thomas à Becket's
shrine, at Canterbury Cathedral in England, were immortalized by the English
poet Geoffrey Chaucer (c. 1345–1400), in his legendary *Canterbury Tales.*

18th-century bronze
horse and rider
from Nigeria
in West Africa

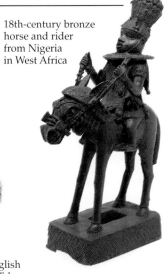

Canvas-covered barrel top

Shaft

Sock

Nine-year-old Irish Draft horse (wearing
traditional Gypsy harness) pulling a Gypsy
caravan, built in Ireland, c. 1850

Horse-drawn vehicles

Snow sled with fur-lined seats for passengers and driver, built in the Netherlands, c. 1880

THE EARLIEST CHARIOTS in the ancient world had solid wooden wheels and a fixed axle that did not pivot. The invention of light, spoked wheels, like those shown here, meant that the chariot, or carriage, could travel much faster. The four-wheeled carriage, with a swiveling axle that could turn independently of the body, was a further improvement that became common only in the early Middle Ages. Just as today people show their status in society by the kind of car they own, in the past they did the same with their horse and carriage. The poor traveled in carts and on horse buses, while the rich traveled in superb carriages harnessed to the most perfect horses. Great effort went into maintaining horses, harnesses, and carriages. Horses had to be fed and fitted with shoes (which is why so many people of English ancestry are called Smith), wheels had to be greased and repaired (giving another surname, Wheeler), and the carriages had to be kept clean and dry.

Bronze model of horse and carriage, Eastern Han dynasty of China, 2nd century A.D.

Elegant and expensive carriage harnessed to a pair of beautifully turned out horses

WHOSE LAND IS IT ANYWAY?
The early European immigrants who traveled across North America by stagecoach were often attacked by Native Americans on horseback, armed with stolen or bartered guns, as depicted in this painting by artist George Inness (1854–1926).

Blinker

Collar

Terret

Crupper

Check or driving rein

Hame

Bit

Martingale

Girth strap

Hip strap

Tongue

Trace

Triple whiffletree connecting two pairs of horses to stagecoach

Only one seat left
on this overcrowded
horse bus – two
people will be
disappointed

Driver's seat

Seating for two passengers

A type of Victorian carriage called a
barouche, made in England based on
a French design, c. 1880

WAY OUT WEST
Two businessmen –
Henry Wells (1805–1878)
and William Fargo
(1818–1881) – opened
their offices in San
Francisco in 1852 to
provide banking and
shipping services, linking
the Far West with the rest
of the nation. The famous
Wells, Fargo stagecoaches
would carry private
passengers, mail,
money, and other
valuables.

Jehu, or driver

Guard-messenger riding shotgun

Extra luggage stowed on top

Roll-up leather curtains to let in cool air or to keep out snow and rain

Brake lever operated by driver's foot

Seating inside for nine passengers – three each on three benches

WELLS FARGO & CO. OVERLAND STAGE

US MAIL

Two sets of reins connecting the two pairs to driver

Passengers' luggage stowed in rear trunk

Step for passengers getting into stagecoach

Box under driver's seat containing tools, water bucket, mail pouches, and strongboxes full of valuables

Standing room for up to 12 passengers

Driver's seat

Two pairs of Welsh Cobs
hauling Wells, Fargo stagecoach,
made in U.S., late 1800s

Hunting brake, with driver's seat
and space for standing room only,
made in England, c. 1880

Heavy horses

In europe and asia, "the age of the horse" lasted from the classical times of Greece and Rome until the beginning of the 19th century. During this long period, until they were overtaken by the steam locomotive, not only were the horse, mule, and donkey the primary means of transportation, they were also necessary for all kinds of agricultural work. They were used for forestry, harvesting, pulling brewers' drays (low carts), and threshing grain, as well as for drawing water from wells. In the Mediterranean and Middle East areas, where the soils are light and dry, the donkey (pp. 24–25) carried out these tasks. In northern Europe, where the soils are damp and full of sticky clay, powerful heavy horses were needed for plowing and hauling heavy loads along muddy roads. Today, the heavy horses of Britain and Europe are exported around the world – to Canada, the U.S., Australia, and Japan.

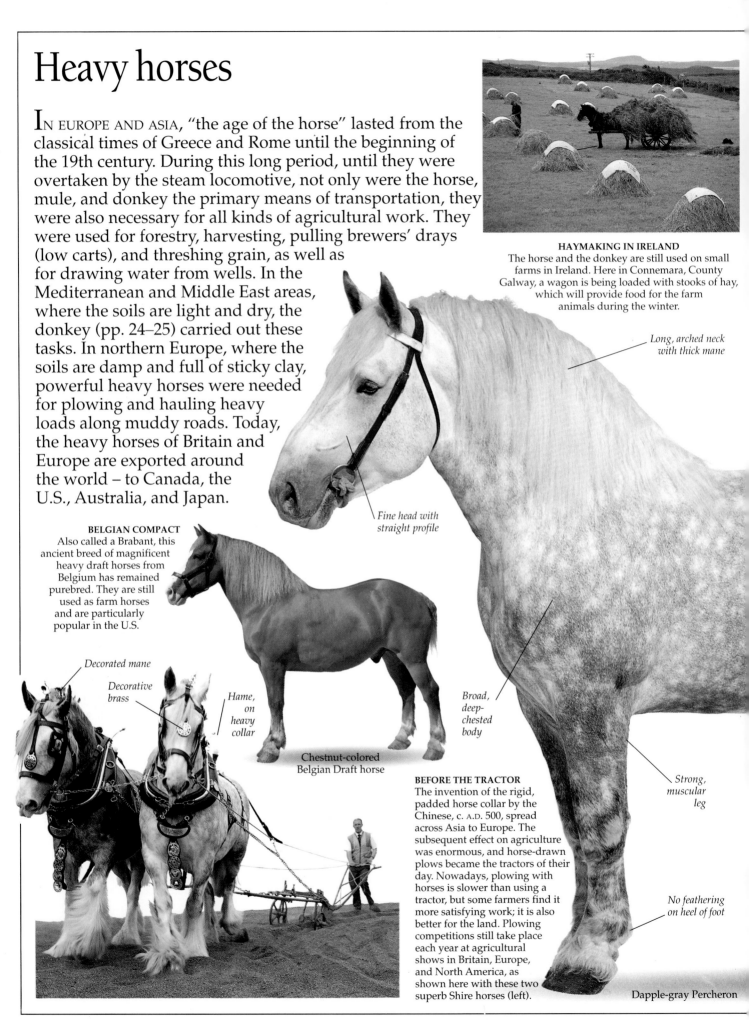

HAYMAKING IN IRELAND
The horse and the donkey are still used on small farms in Ireland. Here in Connemara, County Galway, a wagon is being loaded with stooks of hay, which will provide food for the farm animals during the winter.

Long, arched neck with thick mane

Fine head with straight profile

BELGIAN COMPACT
Also called a Brabant, this ancient breed of magnificent heavy draft horses from Belgium has remained purebred. They are still used as farm horses and are particularly popular in the U.S.

Decorated mane

Decorative brass

Hame, on heavy collar

Chestnut-colored Belgian Draft horse

Broad, deep-chested body

Strong, muscular leg

BEFORE THE TRACTOR
The invention of the rigid, padded horse collar by the Chinese, c. a.d. 500, spread across Asia to Europe. The subsequent effect on agriculture was enormous, and horse-drawn plows became the tractors of their day. Nowadays, plowing with horses is slower than using a tractor, but some farmers find it more satisfying work; it is also better for the land. Plowing competitions still take place each year at agricultural shows in Britain, Europe, and North America, as shown here with these two superb Shire horses (left).

No feathering on heel of foot

Dapple-gray Percheron

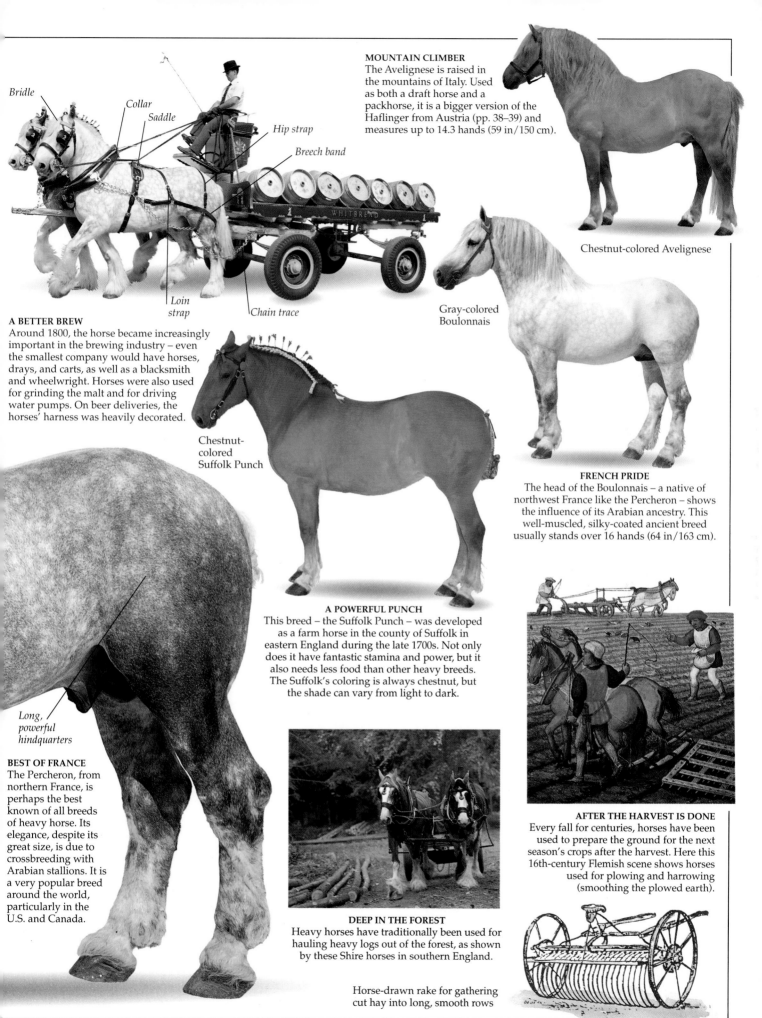

MOUNTAIN CLIMBER
The Avelignese is raised in the mountains of Italy. Used as both a draft horse and a packhorse, it is a bigger version of the Haflinger from Austria (pp. 38–39) and measures up to 14.3 hands (59 in/150 cm).

Chestnut-colored Avelignese

Bridle

Collar

Saddle

Hip strap

Breech band

Loin strap

Chain trace

Gray-colored Boulonnais

A BETTER BREW
Around 1800, the horse became increasingly important in the brewing industry – even the smallest company would have horses, drays, and carts, as well as a blacksmith and wheelwright. Horses were also used for grinding the malt and for driving water pumps. On beer deliveries, the horses' harness was heavily decorated.

Chestnut-colored Suffolk Punch

FRENCH PRIDE
The head of the Boulonnais – a native of northwest France like the Percheron – shows the influence of its Arabian ancestry. This well-muscled, silky-coated ancient breed usually stands over 16 hands (64 in/163 cm).

Long, powerful hindquarters

BEST OF FRANCE
The Percheron, from northern France, is perhaps the best known of all breeds of heavy horse. Its elegance, despite its great size, is due to crossbreeding with Arabian stallions. It is a very popular breed around the world, particularly in the U.S. and Canada.

A POWERFUL PUNCH
This breed – the Suffolk Punch – was developed as a farm horse in the county of Suffolk in eastern England during the late 1700s. Not only does it have fantastic stamina and power, but it also needs less food than other heavy breeds. The Suffolk's coloring is always chestnut, but the shade can vary from light to dark.

AFTER THE HARVEST IS DONE
Every fall for centuries, horses have been used to prepare the ground for the next season's crops after the harvest. Here this 16th-century Flemish scene shows horses used for plowing and harrowing (smoothing the plowed earth).

DEEP IN THE FOREST
Heavy horses have traditionally been used for hauling heavy logs out of the forest, as shown by these Shire horses in southern England.

Horse-drawn rake for gathering cut hay into long, smooth rows

51

Horse power

WITHOUT THE HORSE, the industrial revolution at the end of the 18th century could never have taken place. Horse transportation allowed manufactured goods to be carried to ships for export to foreign countries, and it enabled people to flock to the cities for work in the new industries. Horses were used in the factories to provide power to engines and machines for grinding malt for brewing (pp. 50–51) or wheat for flour, spinning cotton, and furnace blowing. In the mines, ponies were used underground for hauling loads from the coal face (pp. 62–63) and above ground for towing barges full of coal along the canals. Horses also hauled buses, fire engines, and goods wagons. Today, there are few places where the horse has not been replaced by machinery, but the term used to measure the pulling power of an engine is still "horsepower." One horsepower is equivalent to 746 watts, and one metric horsepower equals 736 watts.

Cog

Shaft attached to grinding stones

HORSE BUSES
The first public horse carriages in Britain started in 1564, but the roads were so bad that people could not travel far, especially in winter.

Weighing scales

COAL MERCHANT
THOMAS JEWELL

Heavily laden coal wagon, made in England, 1920

Sack of coal

Brake

SNOWSHOES
In heavy snow, a sturdy team of surefooted horses is needed to haul logs out of forests or sleds full of people or goods, as shown by these Haflinger ponies in Bavaria in southern Germany.

Lamp

Horn

Water hose

LONDON

Water bucket

EXPLORING THE INTERIOR
Teams of horses hauled wood wagons laden with supplies to Australia's interior, such as this area of New South Wales. The safety of these wagons depended on the wheels being made correctly.

Victorian fire engine, English, 1890 – wheels were wide to allow horses to turn corners sharply without risking a spill

Giant iron flywheel attached
to an iron shaft, or rod

GOING AROUND IN CIRCLES
The tediousness of this circular
work is all the more apparent
when viewed from above.

Heavy
collar

Whiffletree
attached to iron
bar, in turn
linked to shaft

Metal linked-
chain trace

Long, well-
muscled leg
helping horse
pull heavy load

Huge, flat grinding
stones hidden
underground

Shire horse pulling heavy horse gin, or horse wheel,
inside a circular building called a roundhouse

TOWING A BARGE
Horses and mules were
often used to pull
barges heavily laden
with coal or farm
produce along rivers
and canals in Great
Britain and Europe – an
efficient means of
transport that lasted
well into the 20th
century.

A HARD GRIND
This horse is being used to turn a mill
wheel to grind corn into flour – just as
horses, mules (pp. 26–27), and donkeys
(pp. 24–25) have done all over Europe
since Roman times. The animals were
forced to walk around and around in a
small circle for hours on end, pulling
the rope or chain that turned the heavy
grinding stone. Sometimes, a pair of
horses would carry out this operation –
they had to be specially trained to keep
to a steady pace and at the correct speed.

Light draft work

THEY MAY NOT BE AS ELEGANT as the Thoroughbred, or as magnificent as the heavy horse, but the common light draft horses were the mainstay of transportation throughout the world until the invention of the steam engine in the 1820s. Light draft horses pulled every kind of wagon, carriage, and cart. These horses had to be powerful and fast, as well as able to cover long distances without becoming tired. Normally, they did not belong to any particular breed, but some – like the Cleveland Bay of Yorkshire, England – had been preserved as pure breeds since ancient times. Originally, Cleveland Bays were known as "Chapman horses" because they were used to carry the loads of traveling salesmen, or "chapmen," around the countryside.

Hansom cab (c. 1850), designed for two passengers, driven by single driver and horse

CROWD CONTROL
The specially trained horses of mounted police still perform an important function in being able to move fast through crowds of people. They provide their riders with mobility and a good view of events.

Feathered plume

PACKHORSE
For centuries, horses have been used for carrying heavy loads on their backs. This woodcutter's horse in Guatemala is laden with planks of wood.

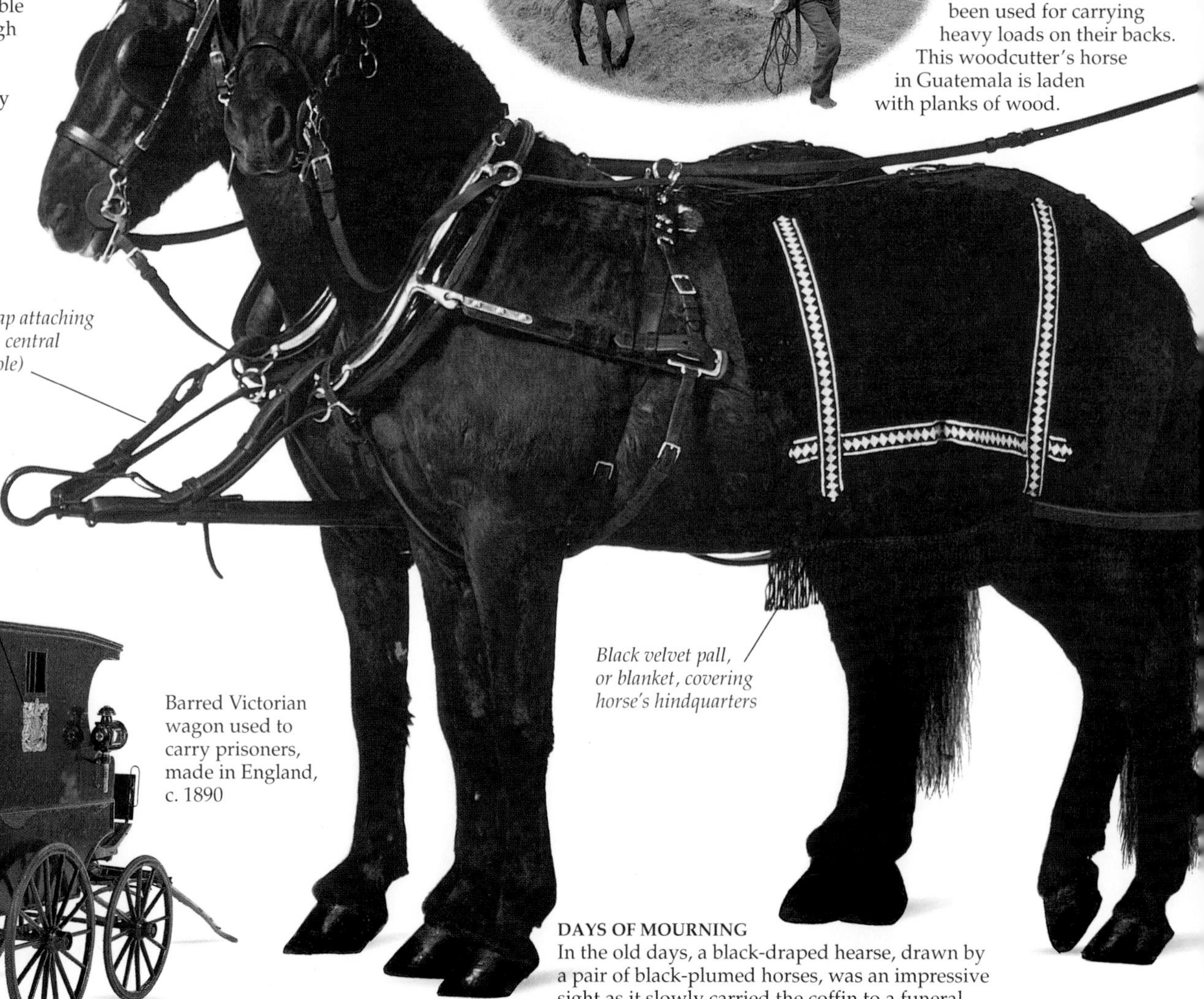

Pole strap attaching collar to central shaft (pole)

Royal coat of arms

Barred Victorian wagon used to carry prisoners, made in England, c. 1890

Black velvet pall, or blanket, covering horse's hindquarters

DAYS OF MOURNING
In the old days, a black-draped hearse, drawn by a pair of black-plumed horses, was an impressive sight as it slowly carried the coffin to a funeral.

SUNDAY MORNING DRIVE
A family enjoys an outing in their horse-drawn carriage in this print by lithographers Nathaniel Currier (1813–1888) and James Ives (1824–1895).

Harness attached to center pole

Pair of grays and phaeton, English, c. 1840

REGENCY RAKE ABOUT TOWN
In English spa towns in the early part of the 19th century, young gentlemen would flit around town driving their latest status symbol, such as this convertible model – an elegant, sporty phaeton driven with the top up or down.

Driver dressed in dark mourning suit

Plumes made of ostrich feathers

Coffin

Engraved glass sides

Splinter bar to which traces are attached

R. JORDAN & SONS
THE PADDOCK

Pair of black Welsh Cobs, in black and silver harness, pulling funeral hearse, made in England, c. 1850

Rubber-wheeled dairy wagon, made in England, c. 1950

The horse in North America

THE INDIGENOUS (NATIVE) WILD HORSES of North America became extinct about 10,000 years ago. The first domestic horses landed on the continent with Christopher Columbus in 1492. Since then horses have symbolized freedom and enterprise in North America, and for the next 425 years the rise in the horse population matched that of the human population. Horses have been used by nearly everyone – they have drawn heavy loads in the searing heat of deserts, down deep mines, and along muddy roads. The horse transformed the lives of Native Americans, who had previously hauled their possessions by dogsled and on their own backs. With the horse, the native peoples had a new means of fast transportation and could also hunt buffalo more efficiently.

BUFFALO BILL
In 1882, former Pony Express rider (pp. 62–63) Buffalo Bill Cody (1846–1917) put on the first professional rodeo show at the Fourth of July celebrations in Nebraska, with contests in shooting, riding, and broncobusting.

TRAVEL TODAY
The Amish settled in Pennsylvania in the early 1700s and developed the Conestoga (a heavier version of the covered wagon), which helped explore the West (pp. 34–35). Today their simple lifestyle means that they still use horses for both work and travel.

A MUSICAL RIDE
The Royal Canadian Mounted Police (founded in 1873) are world famous for their splendid pageantry – red tunics, black horses, and bright banners.

Stetson hat

Fringed leather jacket

Striped saddle-cloth

High pommel of Western saddle

Saddle horn

Stock whip

Flowing mane

Western curb bit

LEGENDARY LADIES
Calamity Jane, Annie Oakley, Belle Starr . . . the list of female legends of the Old West is endless, when cowgirls had to ride a horse, shoot a gun, and cope with everything as well as any man. The bad guys and girls – like Frank and Jesse James, the Dalton gang, Billy the Kid, and Flo Quick – were chased by lawmen like Wyatt Earp and Wild Bill Hickok, and everyone rode a horse.

Leather chaps

Leather stirrups

The Appaloosa, with its distinctive spotted coat (pp. 40–41), was a favorite mount of Native Americans.

Cowgirl in typical Western clothes riding 14-year-old skewbald pony

STAMPEDE!
Every July at the Calgary Stampede in Canada, the contests of skill and speed at this rodeo include the dramatic chuck (food) wagon races. Two pairs of horses, a cook–driver, and four outriders race around a circuit – the first across the finish line wins.

Lasso for roping cattle

Stetson

Saddle horn

Silver and tooled-leather gun belt

HOLLYWOOD HEROES
"There isn't a bronc that can't be rode; there isn't a cowboy that can't be throwed." The central feature of the rodeo show is the bucking horse, symbol of humans' need to conquer the wild and the free, but a horse is not "broken" without a fight. Wild-horse races are also a feature of some rodeos, in which unbroken horses are saddled and ridden to show off the cowboys' courage. Movie cowboys and their famous horses – such as the Lone Ranger and Silver, Roy Rogers and Trigger – helped to recreate the legend of the Old West.

Western curb bit

BUFFALO HUNT
In this painting by artist George Catlin (1796–1872), the Native Americans' horses are shown hunting the buffalo – which all but disappeared from the West through excessive slaughter by European immigrants.

PAUL REVERE'S RIDE
Famous for his ride from Boston on the night of April 18, 1775, to warn the colonists of Massachusetts that the British troops were coming, Paul Revere (1735–1818) and his borrowed horse have become an American legend.

Leather chaps

Leather stirrups

ARMY ROUGHRIDERS
Ordinary cavalrymen (an army's mounted forces) had to spend long hours in the saddle, so it was important to have strong horses. In this painting by artist Frederic Remington (1861–1909), the U.S. Cavalry is in hot pursuit.

Cowboy on palomino (part Thoroughbred, part Arabian)

Sporting horses

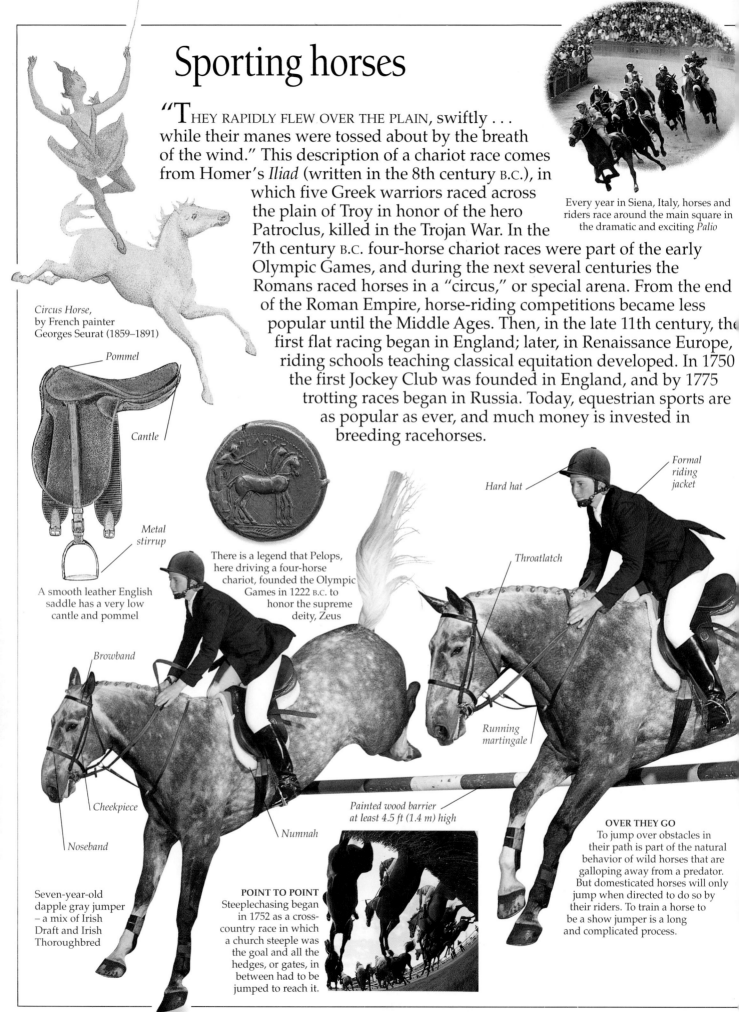

"THEY RAPIDLY FLEW OVER THE PLAIN, swiftly . . . while their manes were tossed about by the breath of the wind." This description of a chariot race comes from Homer's *Iliad* (written in the 8th century B.C.), in which five Greek warriors raced across the plain of Troy in honor of the hero Patroclus, killed in the Trojan War. In the 7th century B.C. four-horse chariot races were part of the early Olympic Games, and during the next several centuries the Romans raced horses in a "circus," or special arena. From the end of the Roman Empire, horse-riding competitions became less popular until the Middle Ages. Then, in the late 11th century, the first flat racing began in England; later, in Renaissance Europe, riding schools teaching classical equitation developed. In 1750 the first Jockey Club was founded in England, and by 1775 trotting races began in Russia. Today, equestrian sports are as popular as ever, and much money is invested in breeding racehorses.

Every year in Siena, Italy, horses and riders race around the main square in the dramatic and exciting *Palio*

Circus Horse, by French painter Georges Seurat (1859–1891)

Pommel

Cantle

Metal stirrup

A smooth leather English saddle has a very low cantle and pommel

There is a legend that Pelops, here driving a four-horse chariot, founded the Olympic Games in 1222 B.C. to honor the supreme deity, Zeus

Hard hat

Formal riding jacket

Throatlatch

Browband

Running martingale

Cheekpiece

Painted wood barrier at least 4.5 ft (1.4 m) high

Numnah

Noseband

Seven-year-old dapple gray jumper – a mix of Irish Draft and Irish Thoroughbred

POINT TO POINT
Steeplechasing began in 1752 as a cross-country race in which a church steeple was the goal and all the hedges, or gates, in between had to be jumped to reach it.

OVER THEY GO
To jump over obstacles in their path is part of the natural behavior of wild horses that are galloping away from a predator. But domesticated horses will only jump when directed to do so by their riders. To train a horse to be a show jumper is a long and complicated process.

58

IN COLD WATER
Three-day eventing tests the endurance, speed, and obedience of a horse, as well as its rider's ability. The event is broken down into dressage on the first day, followed by a cross-country and steeplechase course that includes a spectacular water hazard (as shown), with show jumping on the third and final day.

FUN FOR EVERYONE
Gymkhanas, or mounted games, offer young riders a chance to see what they and their ponies can do at this junior level of equestrian, or horse-riding, competition.

Riding side saddle originated with European royalty some 600 years ago, but in 19th-century England ladies rode this way for the hunt

Saddle horn

High cantle

Lariat

Classic jodphurs, or riding pants

English jumping saddle

Leather stirrup

Western saddles, made of heavy tooled leather, had distinctive pommels (saddle horns) used by cowboys when roping cattle with lariats (lassoes)

Rein

Bridoon

Galloping boots to protect from overreach of hind feet

Girth

Metal stirrup

ANYONE FOR POLO?
Polo, as seen in this 17th-century silk print, was invented by the Chinese about 2,500 years ago. Today it is very popular in Argentina, the U.S., Australia, and Britain. Two teams of four players each hit the ball with long-handled mallets and try to score as many goals as possible in seven and a half minutes (a "chukker"). There can be from four to six chukkers in a match. The team with the most goals wins the match.

THEY'RE OFF!
Modern flat racing – racing on a track with no obstacles – owes its existence to the Thoroughbred (pp. 38–39), first developed in Britain during the 17th and 18th centuries. Today influential racing nations include Britain, France, Italy, Australia, and the U.S.

Horses for courses

THE CLOSE BOND that has been forged over thousands of years between humans and horses cannot be broken by the rise of the automobile. Today the horse is becoming ever more popular in competitive sports, and those who cannot take part in showjumping or racing get much pleasure from watching them on television. Most highly bred horses, in particular those that compete at the highest levels, must be carefully trained to maintain their fitness and optimize their chance of winning. Racehorses will use their natural instincts to follow a leader (the other horses), helped by the sting of a whip. Show jumpers and dressage horses combine training with obedience. Besides racing or jumping, the most ancient sport involving horses is hunting, which many people consider to be cruel to the prey. Horses (singly or in teams) provide an amazing variety of sports and recreation for thousands of people around the world – from pony-trekking and endurance racing to international driving and classical equitation, or dressage.

AWAY TO THE RACES
Flat racing – the "sport of kings" – is very popular around the world in such classic races as England's Derby, America's Belmont Stakes, and Australia's Melbourne Cup. Here the French Impressionist painter Edgar Degas (1834–1917) shows jockeys and horses in their owners' racing colors awaiting their call to the start line.

Height at withers 15 hands (60 in/ 152 cm)

CROSSING A CREEK
All around the world, pony trekking is a popular recreation for both adults and children. In this picture children are riding their ponies in single file across a shallow stream in the Victorian Alps in southeastern Australia.

PACERS AND TROTTERS
In many parts of the world, including North America, France, Russia, Australia, and New Zealand, the trotting or harness race is just as popular as flat racing. The modern trotting race is similar to the ancient chariot race, except that it is run with a single horse that is only allowed to trot. In pacing (as shown here), the legs move in lateral (same side) rather than diagonal pairs (legs move in diagonal pairs for conventional trotting).

THREE HORSEMEN
For centuries, riders took part in long-distance races to see who could break the latest time and distance record. In this 18th-century Japanese print by Katsushika Hokusai (1760–1849), three horsemen are racing to the foothills of Mt. Fuji.

Three-year-old bay American Standardbred driven by owner in his racing colors

ELEGANT DRESSAGE
Classical riding shows the horse at its peak of fitness and its obedience to its rider, and it reached its height of popularity in the 18th century. In modern advanced dressage competitions, marks out of ten are given for excellence. One of the most difficult movements (shown here) is piaffe, in which the horse maintains the beat of a slow, elevated trot without moving forward.

For centuries, horsehair from the horse's tail has been used for stringing bows of musical instruments, such as the cello

THE HUNTERS RETURN
Hunting from horseback has been carried out since the time of the Assyrians, c. 2500 B.C., when the prey was lions or wild oxen. Later, in Europe, as shown in this 16th-century Flemish calendar, the quarry was the stag, bear, or hare. In the 17th century, the English developed fox-hunting with the help of specially trained scent hounds, and it is still occurs there as well as in the eastern US.

HAVE YOU PASSED YOUR DRIVING TEST YET?
At horse shows around the world, driving events are very popular. In 1970 the first international horse driving trials, based on the format of the three-day event, took place. These trials had presentation and dressage on the first day, followed by a marathon of 17 miles (27 km), and then obstacle driving on the final day.

Driving whip

Jockey cap

Shirt showing owner's racing colors

Sulky, or cart

Special harness around legs to help horse maintain its lateral pacing

Walking the horse

The horse has four natural gaits – the walk, trot, canter, and gallop. The walk has four beats – left hind, left fore, right hind, and right fore legs, each hitting the ground separately. The trot has two beats – left hind and right fore together, then right hind and left fore together. The canter has three beats – left hind, then left fore and right hind together, and finally the right fore leg. The gallop has four beats – the same as the walk – then all four feet come off the ground.

Useful ponies

CHILDREN WHO LEARN TO RIDE and care for a pony develop an understanding of the rich relationships that can exist between humans and animals, and a pony can often be a child's best friend. In the past, the native ponies of northern Europe were used as pack animals and for general farm work, and then when a particularly docile pony was too old to work, it was given to a small child for the first riding lessons. In those times almost everyone knew how to handle a horse. Today, fewer people learn to ride and even fewer have a pony of their own, but for those who do, it is a most rewarding experience. Most breeds, like the Dartmoor and Fell ponies, are extremely hardy and have evolved in a harsh environment where they survive on little food and remain outdoors all winter. However, thoroughbred ponies that are trained for the show ring need much more care.

THROUGH ALL KINDS OF WEATHER
From Missouri to California, Pony Express riders braved bad weather, difficult terrain, and attacks from Native Americans to carry the mail 2,000 miles (3,300 km) across the U.S. in the 1860s. They managed to cut delivery time from weeks to just days.

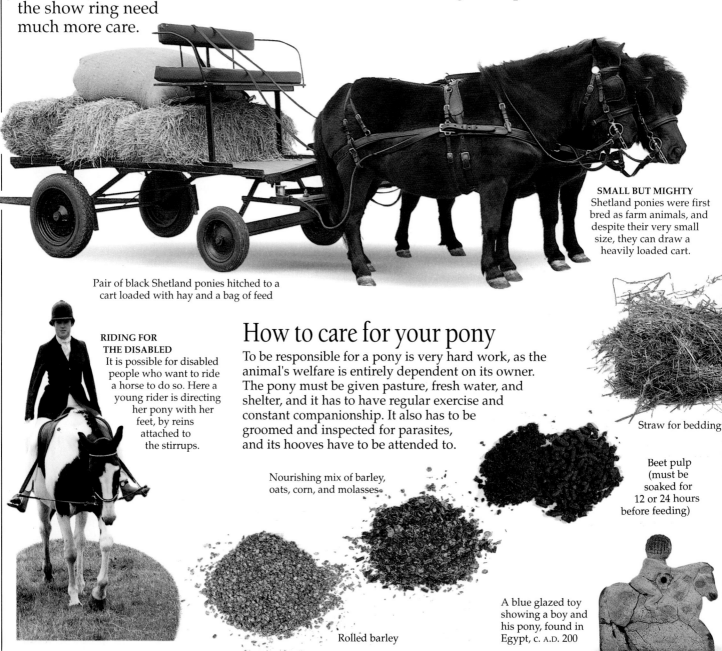

Pair of black Shetland ponies hitched to a cart loaded with hay and a bag of feed

SMALL BUT MIGHTY
Shetland ponies were first bred as farm animals, and despite their very small size, they can draw a heavily loaded cart.

RIDING FOR THE DISABLED
It is possible for disabled people who want to ride a horse to do so. Here a young rider is directing her pony with her feet, by reins attached to the stirrups.

Straw for bedding

How to care for your pony

To be responsible for a pony is very hard work, as the animal's welfare is entirely dependent on its owner. The pony must be given pasture, fresh water, and shelter, and it has to have regular exercise and constant companionship. It also has to be groomed and inspected for parasites, and its hooves have to be attended to.

Beet pulp (must be soaked for 12 or 24 hours before feeding)

Nourishing mix of barley, oats, corn, and molasses

A blue glazed toy showing a boy and his pony, found in Egypt, c. A.D. 200

Rolled barley

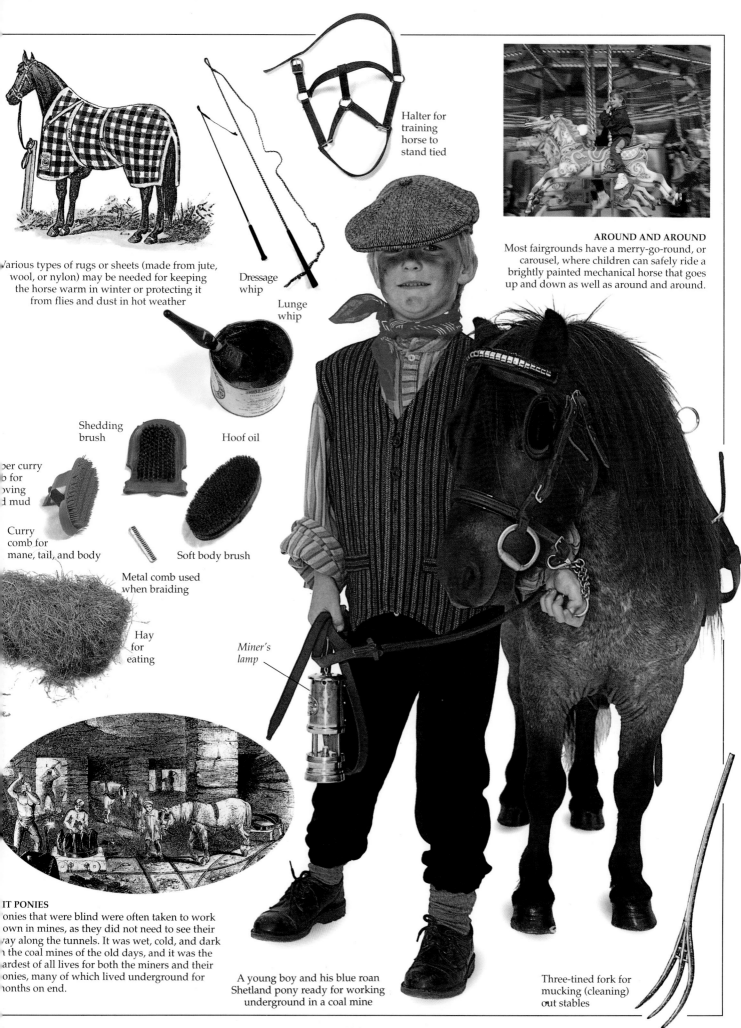

Various types of rugs or sheets (made from jute, wool, or nylon) may be needed for keeping the horse warm in winter or protecting it from flies and dust in hot weather

Dressage whip

Lunge whip

Halter for training horse to stand tied

AROUND AND AROUND
Most fairgrounds have a merry-go-round, or carousel, where children can safely ride a brightly painted mechanical horse that goes up and down as well as around and around.

Shedding brush

Hoof oil

Rubber curry comb for removing dried mud

Curry comb for mane, tail, and body

Soft body brush

Metal comb used when braiding

Hay for eating

Miner's lamp

PIT PONIES
Ponies that were blind were often taken to work down in mines, as they did not need to see their way along the tunnels. It was wet, cold, and dark in the coal mines of the old days, and it was the hardest of all lives for both the miners and their ponies, many of which lived underground for months on end.

A young boy and his blue roan Shetland pony ready for working underground in a coal mine

Three-tined fork for mucking (cleaning) out stables

Did you know?

AMAZING FACTS

The head of this herd of horses is probably a mare.

A horse drinks at least 44 pints (25 liters) of water each day. That's about 13 times as much as an adult human.

Within an hour of being born, a foal is up on its feet and able to walk. It takes a child about a year to master the same skills. In the wild this ability is essential, because the foal has to move on with the rest of the herd.

A herd of horses is usually led by a mare (a female horse). She decides when the herd should move on to look for fresh grazing and also keeps discipline within the herd. She uses behavior like the bite threat (see p.13) to keep the other members of the herd in order.

"Horsepower" is an internationally recognized unit of power. Scientists define it as the power that is required to lift a weight of 163 lbs (75 kg) over a distance of 39 in (1 m) in 1 second. But a real horse is 10 to 13 times as strong as this, so strangely one horse does not equal one horsepower.

People argued for many years about whether a horse takes all four feet off the ground when it gallops. Then in 1872, a photographer called Eadweard Muybridge set up a line of 24 cameras and photographed a horse galloping past. The pictures proved that during each stride a horse does indeed have all four feet off the ground at the same time.

A donkey carrying a load of straw

"Doing the donkey work" means doing hard, boring work. The expression comes from the fact that donkeys were bred for their stamina and endurance and were used mainly to carry heavy loads. More interesting jobs, such as carrying riders, were normally done by horses.

A mother horse and her foal

Horses have powerful lungs and strong hearts to help them run fast. A thoroughbred horse's heart can weigh up to 11 lbs (5 kg). That's about 16 times as heavy as an adult person's heart, which weighs in at a puny 9 oz (300 g).

The Shire Horse is the largest breed of horse. But the biggest ever horse was a Percheron called Dr. Le Gear. He measured an amazing 21 hands (84 in/213 cm) high.

The expression "straight from the horse's mouth" means to hear something directly from the best authority. It comes from the fact that the best way to discover the age of a horse is to examine its teeth. As a horse gets older, its incisor teeth become worn down and protrude out of its mouth more. Horse experts can use these signs to tell how old the horse is.

A 20-year-old horse shows its teeth

QUESTIONS AND ANSWERS

Q Why do newborn foals look so gangly?

A When a foal is born, its legs are already about 90 percent of their adult length, whereas the rest of its body has to grow a lot. This makes it look very gangly. Foals often have to bend their front legs to reach down to eat grass.

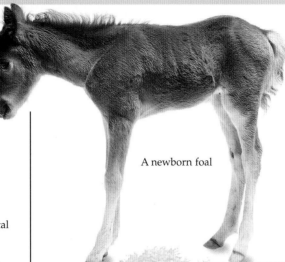

A newborn foal

Q Why are horses' eyes positioned on the sides of their heads?

A This eye position gives the horse good all-around vision, which is vital for spotting potential dangers. When a horse is grazing, it can see all around without having to raise or turn its head.

Q Why do horses often roll on the ground?

A Rolling helps a horse scratch places it can't otherwise reach and shed loose hairs from its coat. Horses from one herd usually roll in the same place. Each horse leaves its individual scent on the rolling patch. These scents gradually mix together to produce a unique "herd smell" that helps the horses in the herd bond together.

A horse rolling

Q Why do horses run away?

A Horses facing danger have two options—fight or flight. They nearly always prefer to run away. One horse in the herd is always on guard. If it senses danger, it alerts the others and then the whole herd will run off. Horses run first and ask questions later!

Q When was horse racing first invented?

A The first records of a ridden race come from the ancient Greek Olympic Games in 624 BCE. It took place over a distance of about 1,313 yds (1,200 m) and the jockeys rode bareback.

Q How fast can a horse run?

A The maximum recorded speed for a galloping horse is 43 mph (69 km/h). This is quick enough to put the horse among the 10 fastest mammals in the world, but it is way behind the fastest animal on earth, the cheetah, which can reach speeds of 65 mph (105 km/h).

Q Why do horses come in so many different shapes and sizes?

A People have created the many different types of horse by selective breeding. This means limiting breeding to selected animals, perhaps by cross-breeding between different types of horse or in-breeding within a family. This is done to achieve a desired shape or skill. For example, some horses have been bred for strength, and others for speed. Gradually, over many years, a variety of distinctive horse and pony breeds have emerged from this process.

Q How did the Przewalski horse get its unusual name?

A The Przewalski horse is named after the man who discovered it—Nikolay Przhevalsky. He was a 19th-century Russian explorer who went on several journeys around east-central Asia, exploring previously little known regions, such as the Tien Shan Mountains and Lake Baikal. Przhevalsky was interested in wildlife and assembled extensive plant and animal collections. His natural history discoveries included the wild camel and the wild horse, which he found in western Mongolia in the 1870s.

Record Breakers

HIGHEST JUMP
The world record for the highest horse jump is 8 ft 1.25 in (2.47 m) by Captain Alberto Larraguibel Morales riding Huaso.

SPEED RECORD
The fastest winner of the Epsom Derby was a horse called Lamtarra, who completed the 1.5-mile (2.4-km) course in just 2 minutes 32.31 seconds in 1995.

BIGGEST BREED
The largest breed of horse is the Shire Horse, which stands 16.2–17.2 hands (65–69 in/165–175 cm) high.

SMALLEST BREED
The smallest breed of horse is the Falabella, which is just 7.5 hands (30 in/76 cm) high. Despite its small size, the Falabella is technically not a pony, but a miniature horse, because it has the characteristics and proportions of a horse.

Shire Horse

Falabella

Identifying breeds

THERE ARE ABOUT 160 DIFFERENT breeds and types of horse around the world. Many breeds were developed for specific purposes, such as riding, farm work, or pulling heavy loads.

PONIES

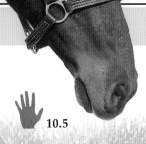

Each horse's height is given in hands (see p. 7), next to the hand symbol.

10.5

AMERICAN SHETLAND
This pony, from the Shetland Islands, was taken to America in 1885 and is now the most popular breed of pony there.

10–12

CASPIAN
The Caspian is the most ancient breed of horse in existence, and may be an ancestor of the Arabian horse.

13–14.2

CONNEMARA
Fast, courageous, and good at jumping, this Irish pony is ideal for competitions.

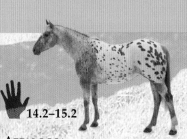

UP TO 13.3

HAFLINGER
The Austrian Haflinger pony is always chestnut or palomino in color with a distinctive flaxen mane and tail.

13–14

FJORD PONY
This Norwegian pony is used for riding, carrying loads, and pulling plows. Its mane is usually cut short.

UNDER 12

WELSH MOUNTAIN PONY
Thanks to its origins in the harsh climate of the Welsh mountains, this hardy pony is able to survive on minimal rations.

RIDING HORSES

14.2–15.2

APPALOOSA
This horse has a distinctive spotted coat. It is descended from horses brought to the Americas by the Spanish conquistadors.

14.2–15

ARABIAN
The Arab is the purest breed of horse. It comes from the Arabian peninsula, where it was in existence as early as 2,500 BCE.

14.2–15

BARB
This breed comes from Morocco, where it was the mount of the Berber horsemen. It is normally gray or black in color.

14.3–16

QUARTER HORSE
This was the first American breed of horse. It was used for farm work and herding cattle and made a perfect cowboy's horse.

15.3–16

SELLE FRANCAIS
This horse's name means "French saddle horse." It was bred for riding, and today is used for show jumping and racing.

16–16.2

THOROUGHBRED
This is the fastest and most valuable of all the breeds of horse. The Thoroughbred is used primarily for racing.

DRIVING HORSES

16–16.2

CLEVELAND BAY
Bred in the northeast of England, the Cleveland Bay was used to carry heavy men out hunting and to pull carriages.

15 AND OVER

FRIESIAN
This horse from the Netherlands was often used to pull funeral carriages because of its black color.

15.2–16.2

GELDERLANDER
Bred specifically to pull carriages, this Netherlands horse is often used in carriage-driving competitions.

15–15.3

HACKNEY
The British Hackney has a distinctive high-stepping gait. It was bred to pull carriages, especially the famous Hackney Cab.

15.1–16.2

LIPPIZANER
The white Lippizaner horse is used at the Spanish Riding School in Vienna, where it excels at displays of dressage.

15.2

STANDARDBRED
This American horse is the world's best breed for harness racing. It can cover a mile (1.6 km) in under two minutes.

DRAFT HORSES

15–16

ARDENNAIS
Originating from the Ardennes region of France and Belgium, this is the oldest of the European heavy breeds.

16.2–17

BELGIAN DRAUGHT
This horse was originally bred for farm work. It has relatively short legs, but is noted for its great strength.

16.2

CLYDESDALE
The Clydesdale originates from Scotland. It was used for pulling heavy loads in cities, particularly brewer's drays.

16.2–17.2

PERCHERON
The French Percheron has been used for many tasks—pulling coaches, farm work, riding, and as a war horse.

16.2–17.2

SHIRE HORSE
The Shire Horse, from the middle shires of England, is the world's largest breed of horse. It was used for pulling plows and other farm work, and in cities for pulling brewer's drays.

Find out more

IF YOU WOULD LIKE TO GET MORE INVOLVED in the world of horses, there are lots of ways to do it. You could start by visiting a horse show—there are many events held around the country in spring and summer, and indoors during the winter—or a county show where many breeds of horse are often on display. If you are feeling more adventurous, why not try riding lessons? Once you have mastered the basics, you will be able to go trekking in the countryside, or even enter a local competition yourself.

ROSETTES
Rosettes are given to the winners in riding competitions. In the United States, blue signifies first place, red second, yellow third, and green fourth. Tricolor rosettes, like this one, are presented for championships.

Tricolor rosette

You must wear a helmet at all times when riding.

VISITING A HORSE SHOW
You can see horses taking part in sports such as show jumping, dressage, and driving events by visiting a horse show. Shows range from small local events, such as a riding club's gymkhana or a local point-to-point (steeplechase), to big county and international shows. The best known are listed in the "Places to Visit" box.

GOING RIDING
If you'd like to try riding, it is important to go to a proper riding school to learn. The Pony Club (www.ponyclub.org) can help you find a stable in your area. You won't need any special equipment, as the school will provide you with a helmet, but it's a good idea to wear long pants and a long-sleeved shirt to protect your skin if you fall off.

Knocking down this pole would incur four faults.

Jodhpurs are more comfortable for riding than ordinary pants.

EQUIPMENT
After two or three lessons, if you decide you want to continue riding, you could invest in some riding clothes. The first and most important things to buy are a helmet and some riding gloves.

Short riding boots or shoes with a heel prevent your feet from slipping through the stirrups.

Pony club silver trophy

Two Camargue horses

All Camargue horses are the same color—gray. Younger animals may be darker, but lighten with age.

SEEING HORSES IN THE WILD
Several breeds of pony live wild in the United States. Two herds make their home on the island of Assateague. The herds, separated by a fence at the Maryland-Virginia state line, can be seen wandering the beaches, roadways, trails, and campgrounds on the island. The small, shaggy horses appear tame, but they are wild and not used to people, so you should be careful not to get too close.

Fly fringes over the horse's ears help to cut out distracting sounds.

Shire Horses pulling a plow

SEEING DIFFERENT BREEDS OF HORSES
Your local county show is a good place to see various types of horses, from ponies to hacks, hunters, and cobs. Larger shows will provide more variety—Stadium Jumping Inc. and Horse Shows In the Sun both give information on where to see shows featuring different breeds from across the country. A large number of breeds are also on display at the Kentucky Horse Park.

Places to Visit

NATIONAL MUSEUM OF RACING AND HALL OF FAME, SARATOGA SPRINGS, NY
www.racingmuseum.org
The museum and hall of fame is across from the historic Saratoga Race Course, the oldest operating track in the United States. The museum houses an equine art collection, trophies, and thoroughbred racing memorabilia.

THE HUBBARD MUSEUM OF THE AMERICAN WEST, RUDOSO, NM
www.hubbardmuseum.com
The museum contains a collection of thousands of horse-related items, including carriages, wagons, horse-drawn vehicles spanning hundreds of years, and facts and artifacts of horse racing's most legendary horses. There are a variety of classes and special events for children, and lectures and educational opportunities for families.

NATIONAL COWBOY AND WESTERN HERITAGE MUSEUM, OKLAHOMA CITY, OK
www.cowboyhalloffame.org
Exhibits include the American Cowboy Gallery and the American Rodeo Gallery. Events include the Chuck Wagon Gathering in May, and the National Children's Cowboy Festival.

THE CHINCOTEAGUE VOLUNTEER FIREMAN'S CARNIVAL, CHINCOTEAGUE, VA
www.chincoteague.com
The main event at the internationally recognized Pony Penning and Auction is watching Assateague Island's wild horses swim across the Assateague Channel to the mainland at low tide. After a rest, the horses are auctioned. The event, each July, attracts thousands of people to Chincoteague, Virginia.

THE KENTUCKY HORSE PARK, LEXINGTON, KENTUCKY
www.kyhorsepark.com/khp/general
A working horse farm where you can see around 50 different breeds of horse. Includes two museums, parade of breeds, and demonstrations of the farrier's skills. The International Museum of the Horse, on park premises, highlights equine works of art and artifacts, and explores equestrian heritage in the United States and abroad.

THE KENTUCKY DERBY MUSEUM
www.derbymuseum.org
New high-tech, hands-on displays and interactive video exhibits bring the Kentucky Derby to life at this museum dedicated to the history of racing.

A racehorse being exercised on Newmarket Heath

Glossary

ARABIAN One of the oldest of all the breeds of horse. Arabian horses originate from the Arabian peninsula, where they were first bred by the Bedouin people around 3,000 years ago.

ASS A member of the horse family. There are two types of ass—the African wild ass (*Equus africanus*) and the Asian wild ass (*Equus hemonius*).

BARB One of the earliest breeds of horse. The barb comes from North Africa, and is the traditional mount of the Berber people.

BIT The part of a bridle that fits in the horse's mouth. Different styles of bit include the snaffle bit, the curb bit, and the pelham (see p. 31).

BLAZE A white marking on a horse's head. A blaze is a wide stripe which starts above the eyes and extends to the muzzle.

BRAND A mark burned on to a horse's skin to show its breed or who owns it

BRIDLE The headgear used to control a horse. A bridle consists of leather straps around the horse's head, a bit in its mouth, and the reins that the rider holds.

BRUMBY A type of feral horse found in Australia. Brumbies are descended from domesticated horses that were abandoned during the gold rushes 150 years ago.

CANTER A gait in which the horse's feet hit the ground in three beats—the left hindleg, then the left foreleg and the right hindleg together, and finally the right foreleg

CAVALRY Soldiers who are mounted on horses

CHIVALRY The combination of qualities expected of an ideal knight in the Middle Ages, such as courage, honor, and courtesy. The term comes from the French word *cheval*, meaning "horse," because knights were mounted soldiers.

COLDBLOODS The name given to an ancient group of horses from northern Europe. Modern-day heavy or draft horses, such as the Shire Horse, Percheron, and Jutland, are believed to have descended from these horses.

African wild ass

Bridle

COLT A male horse that is less than four years old and has not been castrated

CROSS-BRED An animal produced by breeding between two different members of the horse family, or between two different breeds of horse. For example, a mule is bred from a horse and a donkey.

CRUSADES A series of military expeditions made by European knights in the Middle Ages to capture the Holy Land (modern-day Israel) from the Muslims

DOMESTICATION The process of taming a wild animal so that it will live with humans. Horses were first domesticated about 4,000 years ago in eastern Europe.

DONKEY A domesticated ass, descended from the African wild ass (*Equus africanus*)

DRAFT HORSE A horse used for pulling heavy loads and working the land, rather than for riding

DRESSAGE A form of competition in which a rider shows off a horse's skills in obedience and deportment

EQUIDS Members of the horse family of mammals, which includes domestic horses, wild asses, and zebras. The name "equid" comes from *Equidae*, the Latin name for this group of mammals.

EQUITATION The art of horse-riding

FARRIER A person who shoes horses

FERAL An animal that is descended from domesticated ancestors, but has returned to live in the wild. North American mustangs and Australian brumbies are examples of feral horses.

FETLOCK Part of a horse's leg that sticks out just above and behind the hoof. A tuft of hair often grows at the fetlock.

FILLY A female horse that is less than four years old

FLAT RACING Racing horses on a track with no jumps or other obstacles

FORELOCK The tuft of hair that grows on a horse's forehead and falls forward between its ears

GALLOP A fast gait in which the horse's feet hit the ground in four beats, and then all four feet briefly come off the ground at the same time

GAUCHO A cowboy from the South American pampas. Gauchos use horses to round up their cattle.

GELDING A castrated male horse

HAND A unit of measurement used to measure the height of a horse. One hand is 4 in (10.16 cm). A horse's height is measured from the ground to the top of its shoulders.

HARNESS The equipment of straps and fittings by which a horse is fastened to a cart or other vehicle and controlled

HINNY An animal produced by interbreeding between a horse and a donkey. A hinny has a horse father and a donkey mother.

HOOF The horny part of a horse's foot. Hooves are made of keratin, the same substance as human hair and finger nails.

Dressage

Mane

HORSEPOWER A unit of power used to measure the pulling power of an engine. One horsepower is the power required to lift a weight of 163 lbs (75 kg) a distance of 39 in (1 m) in one second.

HOTBLOODS The Thoroughbred and eastern breeds of horse, such as the Arabian and Barb. The name comes from the hot countries of North Africa and Arabia where these breeds originated.

JENNY A female donkey

JOUST A combat between two knights mounted on horses and armed with lances. Jousting was a form of sport invented in the Middle Ages to allow knights to practice their fighting skills without actually killing one another.

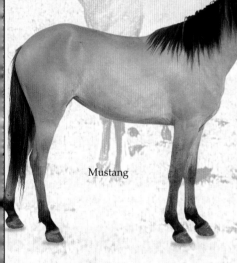

Mustang

LIGAMENT A short band of fibrous tissue that links two bones together and allows a joint to move freely

MANE The long hair that grows from the back of a horse's neck

MARE A female horse who is four or more years old

MULE An animal produced by breeding between a horse and a donkey. A mule has a donkey father and a horse mother.

MUSTANG A type of feral horse found in North America. Mustangs are descended from domesticated horses brought to America at the end of the 15th century by the first European settlers.

MUZZLE A horse's nose and mouth area

ONAGER Another name for the Asian wild ass (*Equus hemonius*)

PACK ANIMAL An animal used to carry loads, rather than for riding. Mules have often been used as pack animals.

PIEBALD A color of horse's coat in which there are large, irregular patches of black and white

POINTS The different external parts of a horse, such as its poll, pastern, withers, and fetlock

PONY A horse that is less than 14.2 hands (58 in/147 cm) high

PRZEWALSKI HORSE The only surviving kind of wild horse. Przewalski horses became extinct in their homeland on the Mongolian steppe during the 1960s, but they are now being reintroduced there from herds bred in captivity.

RODEO A competition in which North American cowboys show off their skills at riding horses and handling cattle

SHOW JUMPING A sport in which horses are ridden around a course which contains a number of fences to jump. The contestants are given penalty points, called faults, for any errors.

SIDESADDLE A position for riding a horse in which both the rider's legs are on the left side of the saddle. In former times, women often rode sidesaddle because their long skirts prevented them from using the normal position, sitting astride the horse.

SKEWBALD A color of horse's coat in which there are large white patches on another coat color

SPUR A U-shaped device with a small spike or wheel attached. Spurs are fitted to the heels of a rider's boots and are used to urge a horse forward.

STALLION A male horse who is four or more years old, and has not been castrated

STEEPLECHASE A race over fences and open ditches. Some courses may also contain a water jump. Traditionally, a steeplechase was a cross-country race from one village to another.

STEPPE A huge grassy plain stretching across Russia and Mongolia. The steppe was once home to herds of wild horses.

STIRRUPS Two leather loops suspended from a horse's saddle with metal footrests to support the rider's feet

STRIPE A white marking on a horse's head. A stripe is a long narrow strip which extends from above the eyes to the nostrils.

A South American spur

TERRET A ring on a saddle harness through which the driving reins pass

THOROUGHBRED A horse whose ancestry can be traced back to one of three famous stallions—the Byerley Turk, the Darley Arabian, or the Godolphin Arabian

TRACE Each of the two side straps or chains by which a horse pulls a vehicle

TROT A gait in which the horse's feet hit the ground in two beats—the left hind and right foreleg together, then the right hind and left foreleg together

WALK A slow, four-time gait in which each of the horse's legs hits the ground separately

WARMBLOODS A name used to describe breeds of horse which are crosses between hotbloods and coldbloods. The Trakehner and the Hanoverian are examples of warmbloods.

WHIPPLETREE A crossbar used to attach a horse's harness to a wagon

WITHERS The top of a horse's shoulders

ZEBRA A member of the horse family, found in Africa, which has a coat patterned with black and white stripes

Przewalski horses

Index

Acknowledgments

The publisher would like to thank:
Alan Hills, Dave Gowers, Christi Graham, Sandra Marshall, Nick Nicholls, and Barbara Winters of the British Museum, and Colin Keates of the Natural History Museum for additional special photography. Clubb Chipperfield Limited, Foxhill Stables & Carriage Repository, Suzanne Gill, Wanda Lee Jones of the Welshpool Andalusian Stud, Marwell Zoological Park, the National Shire Horse Centre, Harry Perkins, and the Whitbread Hop Farm for lending animals and vehicles for photography.
The Household Cavalry for providing the rider and the drum horse, and The Knights of Arkley for the jousting sequence.
The Berrriewood Stud Farm, Carol Johnson, and Plough Studios for their help in providing arenas and studios for photography.
Dr. Alan Gentry of the Natural History Museum, Christopher Gravett of the Royal Armouries (HM Tower of London), and Rowena Loverance of the British Museum for their research help.
Céline Carez, Hannah Conduct, Liz Sephton, Christian Sévigny, Helena Spiteri and Cheryl Telfer for editorial and design assistance.
Jane Parker for the index.
Kim Bryan for editorial consultancy.
Illustrations: John Woodcock

Picture credits
t=top, b=bottom, c=center, l=left, r=right
Aerofilms: 21tl
Allsport: 58tr Vandystadt; 59br Ben Radford
American Museum of Natural History: 8cl, 9br
Ardea: 14clt, 14cl, 16c, 17cr Jean-Paul Ferreo; 17bl Joanna van Grusen
Barnaby's Picture Library: 43cr, 45bl
Bridgeman Art Library: 41tl Archiv fur Kunst & Geschichte, Berlin; 34bl Biblioteca Nacional, Madrid; 24tr, 51cbr, 60c British Library; 49tl Guildhall Library; 39cb Harrogate Museums and Art Galleries; 35t, 41tl, 56tl, 59tc Private Collection; 57ct Smithsonian Institution, Washington, D.C.; 32bl Musée Condée, Chantilly; 58tl (detail) Musée d'Orsay, Paris; 60tr (detail) Louvre, Paris
Trustees of the British Museum: front cover tl, 4ctr, 7br, 16tl, 17br, 22tl, 22cl, 22br, 23tr, 26c, 28c, 33tr, 33bl, 46bl
Bruce Coleman Ltd: 12bl C. Hughes; 18b J. & D. Bartlett; 39tl C. Henneghien
Mike Dent: front cover cr, 23tl, 27tl, 46ctl, 50tr, 54cl, 63tr
Dorling Kindersley: 37tr Dave King (by courtesy of the National Motor Museum, Beaulieu); front cover, 27tr, 36tl, 38 (all except 38br), 40bl, 41 (all except 41tl, 41br), 50c, 50–51b, 51tr, 51c, 51cr, 56bl, 63bc Bob Langrish
Mary Evans Picture Library: 23bl, 32tr
Robert Harding Picture Library: 21cr, 24cb, 48tr, 51bc, 56cr
Alan Hills: 20bl
Hirmer: 33tl
Michael Holford: 31tc, 44tl, 47tc, 59bl, 60bl
Hulton Picture Collection: 53b, 63bl
Kentucky Horse Park, U.S.A 67cb;
Frank Lane Picture Agency: 12bc
Jim Lockwood, Courage Shire Horse Centre, Berks. 67bl;
Bob Langrish: 13c, 20bl, 37tl, 40br, 41br, 54cr, 56cl, 57t, 58bc, 59tl, 59tr, 61tl, 61tc, 65br, 66–67
The Mansell Collection: 42bl
Peter Munt, Ascot Driving Stables, Berks 67tr;
Prince D'elle, Haras National De Saint Lo, France. 66bc;
Natural History Photographic Agency: 14br Patrick Fagot; 21br E. Hanumantha Rao; 36bl, 60cl A.N.T.
Peter Newark's Western Americana: 34tr, 34cl, 43tl, 48cb, 55tl, 57cb, 57bl, 62t
Only Horses: 37c, 62bl
Oxford Scientific Films: 17tc/Anup Shah/Okapia
Planet Earth: 19br Nick Greaves
Pegas of Kilverstone, Lady Fisher. Kilverstone Wildlife Park, Norfolk. 65br;
Spinway Bright Morning, Miss S. Hodgkins, Spinway Stud, Oxon 66tr.
Ann Ronan Picture Library: 6tr
The Board of Trustees of Royal Armouries: 2c, 43cl, 45tc, 45cr
Whitbread Brewery: 13cr
Zefa: 12tr, 13tr, 24clt, 24bl, 25cr, 35br, 36cl, 46cb, 52cl, 52br

Jacket images:
Front: Torleif Svensson